S0-BSK-132

What people are saying about ...

BURY YOUR ORDINARY

"Justin Kendrick masterfully resurrects the vision and practices of discipleship in *Bury Your Ordinary*. This book gives the reader very clear and practical ways to bring Christ to life in our everyday existence. It is the kind of book you will read, put into practice, and then share with others."

Dave Ferguson, lead pastor of
Community Christian Church, author
of *B.L.E.S.S.!* and *Exponential*

"The church in North America is so in need of effective road maps that guide us in what effective and practical discipleship looks like. What does it mean to apprentice ourselves to Jesus, our Messiah and Lord? What does it look like to raise up a generation of Jesus followers who can withstand the cultural and spiritual headwinds we're facing with joy, grace, and spiritual power? My friend Justin Kendrick has given us a great gift in *Bury Your Ordinary*. He's lived out and field-tested what he shares and is seeing 'fruit that remains.' It is possible for believers new and old to grow in maturity and become active participants in helping the kingdom flourish, even in these challenging times. I highly recommend this book to pastors and leaders of all kinds who long to see our churches grow and thrive."

Kevin Palau, president of Luis Palau Association

"This book is for anyone who wants more—more than the mundane life, more than a Sunday kind of faith, more than the ordinary grind. A perfect blend of biblical truth and practicality, Justin's words are both timely and timeless. It is packed with invitations to keep coming back to the pages, keep expanding your relationship with God, and keep expecting the extraordinary in your daily life as you put these essential habits into practice. I can't wait to see the lives that are transformed because of the pages of this book."

Hannah Brencher, author of *Fighting Forward* and *Come Matter Here*

"I thoroughly enjoyed the simplicity, practicality, and reproducibility of Justin's approach to discipleship. He speaks from the perspective of a fellow struggler, not an expert, and helps the ordinary person take steps toward the extraordinary life that God desires for everyone who chooses to follow Jesus."

Scott Ridout, president of Converge

"Justin Kendrick breaks down and makes palatable a topic that, for a long time, has seemed to be a mystery in the body of Christ—DISCIPLESHIP. *Bury Your Ordinary* is a masterpiece and a comprehensive blueprint on discipleship. As you read this book, you will receive precept upon precept on the 'whys' and the 'how-tos' of discipleship. But beyond that, you will receive an impartation of the same passion and zeal for discipleship that is burning in Justin. I've had the privilege of knowing Justin for over twenty years. I have witnessed firsthand how effectively Justin and his team have discipled people and built one of the greatest churches in New England. This is not just any book. It's an inside look into the life of a true disciple of Jesus—one who disciples multitudes!"

Zenzo Matoga, lead pastor of
Impact Church, Boston, MA

"In *Bury Your Ordinary*, Justin's passion for and hands-on experience with discipleship converge into a practical guide for how discipleship can happen in the real world. This book won't make you comfortable, and it won't always be fun—but it will work! If you truly want to learn how someone can be discipled into a deeper relationship with Jesus, this book was written for you!"

Joshua Gagnon, lead pastor of Next
Level Church, author of *It's Not Over*

"In these pages, you will find an accessible, engaging, paradigm-shifting road map to the spiritual life that you've always longed to experience but have often struggled to find. Justin invites us to move beyond spiritual checklists and guilt-ridden growth models to discover an extraordinary and abundant life in Christ."

Todd Mullins, senior pastor of
Christ Fellowship Church

BURY YOUR ORDINARY

PRACTICAL HABITS OF A HEART FULLY ALIVE

JUSTIN KENDRICK

DAVID **C** COOK

transforming lives together

BURY YOUR ORDINARY
Published by David C Cook
4050 Lee Vance Drive
Colorado Springs, CO 80918 U.S.A.

Integrity Music Limited, a Division of David C Cook
Brighton, East Sussex BN1 2RE, England

The graphic circle C logo is a registered trademark of David C Cook.

All rights reserved. Except for brief excerpts for review purposes,
no part of this book may be reproduced or used in any form
without written permission from the publisher.

The website addresses recommended throughout this book are offered as a
resource to you. These websites are not intended in any way to be or imply an
endorsement on the part of David C Cook, nor do we vouch for their content.

Details in some stories have been changed to protect the identities of the persons involved.

Unless otherwise noted, all Scripture quotations are taken from the ESV® Bible (The
Holy Bible, English Standard Version®), copyright © 2001 by Crossway, a publishing
ministry of Good News Publishers. Used by permission. All rights reserved. Scripture
quotations marked THE MESSAGE are taken from THE MESSAGE. Copyright © by
Eugene H. Peterson 1993, 2002. Used by permission of Tyndale House Publishers,
Inc.; NASB are taken from the New American Standard Bible®, copyright © 1960,
1995 by The Lockman Foundation. Used by permission. (www.Lockman.org);
NIV are taken from THE HOLY BIBLE, NEW INTERNATIONAL VERSION®,
NIV® Copyright © 1973, 2011 by Biblica, Inc.® Used by permission. All rights
reserved worldwide; and NLT are taken from the Holy Bible, New Living Translation,
copyright © 1996, 2015 by Tyndale House Foundation. Used by permission
of Tyndale House Publishers, Inc., Carol Stream, Illinois 60188. All rights
reserved. The author has added italics to Scripture quotations for emphasis.

Library of Congress Control Number 2020942524
ISBN 978-0-8307-8118-8
eISBN 978-0-8307-8119-5

© 2021 Justin Kendrick
Published in association with The Bindery Agency, www.TheBinderyAgency.com.

The Team: Michael Covington, Jeff Gerke, Jack Campbell,
James Hershberger, Susan Murdock
Cover Design: Madison Copple
Author Bio Photo: Ian Christmann

Printed in the United States of America
First Edition 2021

1 2 3 4 5 6 7 8 9 10

060921

CONTENTS

PART 4: LONG HAUL LIVING

*For more, including
group study material, visit
BuryYourOrdinary.com.*

FOREWORD

How long does it take to become a Christian? A moment and a lifetime. There is a moment, that we often refer to as conversion, where you are born again. In that moment you are as saved as you are ever going to be. In that moment, the Bible says that you moved from spiritual death to spiritual life. Another Bible passage says that you are transferred from the kingdom of darkness into the kingdom of light. It is not a stretch to say that is the most important moment of your life. It not only changes everything in this life, but it changes everything in the life after this life.

But you will spend your entire lifetime on this planet learning how to live like a Christian. It is a process that theologians call *sanctification*, which refers to the lifelong journey of becoming like Jesus. As Martin Luther said, "A Christian is never in a state of completion, but always in the process of becoming."[1]

There is no simple formula for "becoming." There isn't a one-size-fits-all strategy for discipleship. It would be so much easier if we could just climb up on a spiritual conveyor belt and on the other end we would come out fully baked and fully mature.

But discipleship doesn't work that way. Life doesn't work that way. Making a disciple is much like rearing a child. In fact, I believe the most powerful metaphor for discipleship in the New Testament is the parent-child relationship. In 1 Thessalonians 2, the apostle Paul said to those first-century Christians that he was like a mother to them, nurturing and caring for them. Just a couple of verses later, he said that he was like a spiritual father encouraging, comforting, and urging them in their following of Jesus. Parenting and discipling are way more art than science. While there are some standard best practices of parenting, each child is unique and requires some customization to help them grow to maturity. The same is true for discipleship.

Discipleship, spiritual formation, following Jesus, spiritual growth, or whichever buzz phrase you prefer has been a hot topic among Christian leaders in this generation. It seems as though everyone is trying to crack the code on how to make authentic disciples. I often ask myself and other Christian leaders, "If we actually made a disciple, how would we know it? And what are the strategies or practices that help someone become a mature follower of Jesus?"

Those questions flow out of my own personal journey as a follower of Jesus. I was twelve years old when I experienced the "moment" of conversion. My family was very involved in a Bible-believing, evangelical church. Looking back, I would describe my church's attempt to disciple me as mostly behavior modification. Do the right things and stop doing the wrong things. I was trained to adopt a set of behaviors that reflect how a good Christian lives. It was the perfect recipe for the making of a Pharisee. But the process of "becoming" more and more like Jesus would have been foreign to me.

I carried this struggle into my role as a pastor. I was preaching biblical sermons, and we had lots of good programs and classes and retreats and seminars and trainings. And yet it seemed like the people in my church were stuck spiritually, not making much progress as disciples. For all the effort, time, energy, and resource that we threw at doing church, it seemed like our return on investment was low. We didn't have many believes who had twenty years of growth, but we had plenty of one-year-old Christians who had lived the same year twenty times.

I would have loved to have gotten my hands on a book like *Bury Your Ordinary*. Not only would it have been a huge help for my personal followership of Jesus, but it would have also been invaluable to me as a leader and pastor.

I have had the privilege of knowing Justin Kendrick for several years now. I don't say this lightly: he is one of the most gifted leaders I have been around in my forty-plus years of ministry. He is wise beyond his years, has great faith, authentically shepherds his own family, and has a deep love for Jesus and the church.

One of the best things about *Bury Your Ordinary* is that every page was birthed out of Justin's life and experience (both as a Christ follower and as a pastor). Not only is he personally modeling these truths, but it is bearing great fruit in his church. The ROI is high.

Justin has done a masterful job of creating a framework of habits that if integrated into your life will result in significant spiritual growth. His approach is simple, but not simplistic. The concepts and practices are easy to grasp, but if you are looking for an easy button for discipleship, this is not your book. One feature I love about *Bury Your Ordinary* is that it is challenging and inspiring but it feels doable. This book is not for the faint of heart, but if you are looking for a strategy that will produce true, noticeable fruit in your life, then read on!

If you are weary of being stuck spiritually, this book is for you. If you are looking for a biblical but doable discipleship strategy for your church, this book is for you. If you are tired of spiritually living the same year over and over, it is time to bury your ordinary and begin to experience the life you long to live.

Lance Witt
Founder and leader of Replenish Ministries

INTRODUCTION

I was seventeen years old, sitting on a double-decker bus in Chicago, when God spoke the words that would change my life. It was the second day of a college weekend at a well-known Christian university, and I was hoping to finalize my plans for what I would do after high school. This college had everything I was looking for: courses that interested me, a student body I connected with, and a city that was buzzing with opportunity. I was sitting with a couple of friends I had made over the weekend, each sharing how committed they were to attending the school. Then they turned to me.

"What about you, Justin? Are you going to come here next year?"

That was when God interrupted. I didn't hear an audible voice. I didn't see a flash of lightning. But I did hear something deep inside, almost an inner voice, nudging me in a different direction: *Go home and learn to make disciples.*

What? Go home and do *what*? It seemed crazy. I wasn't even sure what that meant. Yet something inside of me knew what God was calling me to do. I looked up at the Chicago sky and took a deep breath.

"Actually, I don't think so," I said. "I think I need to go home … to … *make* disciples …"

Within a few months, I had enrolled at a state university near my house and had begun a ministry apprenticeship at my local church. People would ask me what my major was at school, and technically I was getting a degree in social work, but I'd sometimes tactlessly answer with an addendum and say, "Truthfully, I'm going to college because I'm trying to figure out how to make disciples." Most people had no idea how to respond. The conversation would usually trail off or abruptly move in a different direction.

I led a few other students to faith in Jesus my first semester, then moved into a dorm on campus and shared a room with three of my new friends. By my senior year, I was living with nine guys in a two-bedroom apartment, all young in faith and learning together to follow Jesus. This was discipleship by trial and error, with a little more error than anything else.

Discipleship is one of those words that Christians use, but it often seems we don't know exactly what it is or how to do it. We know that to be a disciple means to follow Christ, but if we're honest, we aren't completely sure what a disciple actually does or how disciple-making happens. If you ask a mature Christian at your church to "disciple you," he or she will usually meet you for coffee, listen to your problems, and encourage you to read the Bible. Those are all really good things. But is that all there is to discipleship?

How do we live as disciples of Jesus? And how do we leverage our lives to disciple others? Beneath the surface of those questions is another even larger question: How does spiritual growth really work?

This book is the outworking of what I've discovered in the twenty years since that night in Chicago. It is imperfect and incomplete. But it's been tested in the laboratory of real life—first in my own, then in a small group of friends, and finally with thousands of people in a local church context. The results have been nothing short of miraculous. I've had a front-row seat to watch as Christians have seen significant spiritual growth in a short time. Many have finally broken free from destructive patterns, discovered a clearer sense of God's will, and experienced the joy of answered prayer.

Discipleship doesn't need to be a mystery. We can actually create a road map to get us to the destination of spiritual maturity.

When God commanded Adam and Eve to subdue the earth, he gave them authority over creation, but he left a lot of the details for them to discover themselves (Genesis 1:28). He gave no instruction on how to plant corn or herd sheep. He didn't tell them that cotton would be good for making clothes or that cow's milk would be good for drinking. God gave the raw materials to the human race, expecting us to identify and develop systems and routines that produce positive results. It's true that Adam and Eve couldn't make the corn grow, but they could plant the seeds that would lead to a harvest.

In the same way, when Jesus commanded his followers to go and make disciples, he seemed to intentionally leave out some specifics (Matthew 28:19). How exactly do we make a disciple? What do we focus on first? It's true that ultimately all spiritual growth comes from God, but Jesus has given us the raw materials for growth, and he expects us to create the systems and routines that maximize our potential.

This book is a collection of seven spiritual habits. A habit is an acquired pattern of behavior that, when followed regularly, becomes almost involuntary. You've probably had the experience of jumping into your car to run an errand, only to realize that you've somehow taken the route to get to your office instead of the store. It happened without you even thinking about it. This is the power of a habit. If the seven practices described in this book become *habitual*, the spiritual growth that results from them can be exponential.

The first chapter is dedicated to trying to understand the struggle so many Christians are having with spiritual growth. We want to move ahead in our faith but often feel stuck. Next, we'll dissect how growth actually happens according to Scripture. On that foundation, we will build seven spiritual habits, each one building upon the last. (And for more resources, including group study material, check out BuryYourOrdinary.com.)

Before we jump in, let me give you a word of caution from my own life: these habits make me uncomfortable. They challenge my routines, stretch my comfort zones, and nudge me beyond what seems *ordinary* in the Christian life. But if there's one thing we know for certain, it's that the God of the Bible constantly pushes people beyond the ordinary.

This book isn't about adding a few spiritual routines into your already busy life. Rather, it's a field manual to an entirely different way of life in which you dig a deep hole, put the *ordinary you* inside it, cover it with dirt, and walk away. To practice these habits fully, you must bury your ordinary.

Let this serve as an invitation: if you have grown tired of dull spiritual routines and recognize in your heart a hunger for something more, this book is for you. My prayer is that God would use it as fuel on a fire.

Habit: [**hab**-it] *noun:* an acquired
behavior pattern regularly followed until
it has become almost involuntary.

PART 1: TIME FOR A CHANGE

"It's kind of fun to do the impossible."[2]

Walt Disney

"The only greatness for man is immortality."[3]

James Dean

"Come, follow me."

Jesus (Matthew 4:19 NIV)

Chapter One

THE ACHE TO BE GREAT

Greatness redefined as relationship with God

"Do you not know that in a race all the runners run, but only one gets the prize? Run in such a way as to get the prize."

1 Corinthians 9:24 NIV

Stan is forty-eight years old and has bounced around between a few churches over the past ten years. He plays bass guitar on the worship team and volunteers with the students for winter camp. He loves God, prays every day, and usually puts money in the basket on Sundays. He doesn't have any really close friends, and he's never told his wife about his occasional struggle with porn. He hesitates to let anyone in on a deeper level. Stan is a good guy, and he wants to grow spiritually. It's just that his brand of spirituality is … well … *safe*.

Andre is thirty-two and single. He tries to spend time regularly reading the Bible but often finds himself getting distracted or sucked into the world of social media. Andre lives in the city and stays busy with a thousand hobbies. He dates on and off and always seems to be on the go. He goes to church but recently has found himself inventing excuses to sleep in on Sunday. His spiritual life is lingering in the background of his schedule, but it seems to lack any real initiative. He believes in Jesus, but the fire in his eyes is pretty dim. He does the things that Christians do, but underneath the routine, Andre is … well … *bored*.

Monica is twenty-eight and the mother of two little kids. She runs from preschool to gymnastics and rarely has a moment when someone isn't crying or pooping. She fell in love with Jesus when she was in college and even dreamed of moving to the mission field one day, but then she met her husband and adjusted the plan. Those days of big dreams and excitement on a global scale feel like a lifetime ago. Monica talks to God in the margins of her chaotic days, and her faith feels … well … *ordinary*.

Have you ever imagined yourself being a part something really significant? Have you ever written down a dream or a prayer that feels a thousand miles out of reach? There's something inside all of us that desires *more*. We can't completely escape the feeling, but it seems that life often distracts us from directly pursuing the dream. Things pile up and plans change.

These days, maybe you sell homeowner's insurance. Of course, there's nothing wrong with that. It could be a great job that provides for your family. But maybe it's not the dream that's been whispering to your heart for years. Now all you find yourself doing is going through the motions: you finish that college course or you get married and start having kids or you climb the corporate ladder. You love your friends and your family. You even love your church. But it feels as though something important is missing from the equation.

Is it possible that a little honest reflection would confirm that your spiritual life is safe, a little boring, and … well … ordinary? Though that quiet whisper is always in the background, you can't seem to get rid of it.

There's got to be more than this.

I recently came across the obituary of Victor Dorman. I never met him personally, but the final words written about him caught my attention.

> Victor Dorman, who helped change the way Americans buy cheese by putting "the paper between the slices" as chairman of the Dorman Cheese Company, died on March 4 at his home in Delray Beach, Fla. He was 80.[4]

To be honest, I appreciate the paper between the slices of cheese as much as anyone. Mr. Dorman appeared to be a successful businessman and may have been a wonderful person. But when I look back at my life and think about someone writing the two final sentences about my existence on Earth, do I want something like this mentioned?

Are you content with the life you're living? Are you content with your current experience of God, or is something on the inside calling you further? Too often, our reaction to this sense of discontentment is to try to satisfy spiritual desires with natural solutions. We tell ourselves that if we just got the right job or met that special someone or had a baby, then life would feel significant. But regardless of how wonderful these things may be, they cannot satisfy the deeper call of the soul.

. . . .

Regardless of how wonderful these things may be, they cannot satisfy the deeper call of the soul.

. . . .

The early church father Augustine got it right when he prayed, "You have made us for yourself, O Lord. And our hearts are restless until they find their rest in you."[5] Have you felt the stirring of a restless heart? It may be hiding under a thick layer of Netflix, new gadgets, and a recent failed attempt at romance—but it's still there under the surface.

How do we actually experience a life full of adventure, purpose, and power? Is that even possible ... or is this all there is?

Remembering Mr. Magic

On my fifth birthday, my parents threw me a party and invited Mr. Magic to our house. In real life, he was a retired art teacher from the neighboring town, but in my mind, Mr. Magic was a sign and a wonder. He had a black top hat, a white cane, and a box full of mysterious things.

At one point in his performance, he dragged me onto his stage (also known as the corner of my living room) and in front of all my friends asked me to stuff his magical handkerchief in the front of my pants. I was wearing my karate suit and quickly obeyed his instructions. He waved his wand, then pulled the handkerchief out. It now had a large pair of white underwear attached to it. The crowd let out an audible "Ahhhhh."

I was stunned. I immediately checked to see if my underwear was still on, and it was! My mind began racing with possible explanations for what had just happened. The underwear now attached to the hand-kerchief was far larger than anything I had ever worn. I tried to put the pieces together. Somehow, Mr. Magic had replicated my underwear, increased the size of the new pair, and removed it from my body—all in an instant! Amazing. But how did he do it?

At that moment, I was open to any explanation. My five-year-old mind was like a blank sheet of paper. Maybe his wand had underwear-multiplying capabilities. Maybe the handkerchief was made of some super-special material. Maybe my karate suit had magical powers. At that time in my life, at that moment, the concept of *possibility* was completely pliable.

Life would later teach me that magic wands don't exist, that there are no super-special materials, and that my karate suit was just a $19.99 purchase from Walmart. The magic of what's possible got snuffed out by what's reasonable, and Mr. Magic turned back into a retired art teacher from the neighboring town.

Do you remember your days of imagination? In your wildest, most cherished childhood dreams, what did your future look like? Were you an astronaut? A professional athlete? A movie star? I remember dream-ing about being a sailor who would sail a ship around the whole world. I'm sure you had a dream too. But as we got older, we all learned to anchor our dreams in reality. We looked around us and began to expect only what we'd seen others achieve.

This is where the life of Jesus abruptly interrupts our settle-for-less, realistically sized dreams. The accounts of his life describe a man who was constantly stretching the bounds of what was possible. He walked on water, raised the dead, talked to a storm, and cast out demons. In the gospel of Mark, Jesus was confronted by a man whose son was plagued with seizures. The father was desperate for help and cried out to Jesus, "If you can do anything, have compassion on us and help us" (Mark 9:22). The response of Jesus was startling. "'If you can'! All things are possible for one who believes" (Mark 9:23).

What are we supposed to do with a sentence like that? *All things are possible*? Come on, Jesus; let's be realistic! But he didn't stop there.

"Truly, I say to you, whoever says to this mountain, 'Be taken up and thrown into the sea,' and does not doubt in his heart, but believes that what he says will come to pass, it will be done for him" (Mark 11:23).

In another instance, he said, "Very truly I tell you, whoever believes in me will do the works I have been doing, and they will do even greater things than these, because I am going to the Father" (John 14:12 NIV).

The more I study the life of Jesus, the more convinced I am that he wasn't kidding. He was declaring war on our rational, limited view of reality and demanding that we redraw the lines of what is possible. He doesn't want us to believe that only *he* can do impossible things. He wants us to live as though *we* can do them too.

Jesus invites every believer into something more. More than routines, more than deadlines, more than ordinary. Inside every human being, God has put an *ache to be great*, and the Spirit of Jesus calls each of us to respond.

True Greatness

What does it really mean to be great? The world around us is quick to paint a vivid picture. Our culture teaches us that if you acquire a large pile of money or become famous and well known in society, if you have millions of followers on social media—then you are great. We are told that if you accomplish a noteworthy task or invent something new, if you excel as an athlete, if you get your name in the newspaper, or if you win a special award—then you are great. All of these ideas are shadows of the truth, and they don't capture the real essence of greatness.

If this life is all there is, then we could define greatness by these measurements, but the central message of Jesus is that *this life is not all there is!* You are an eternal being, with an eternal purpose. Beyond what you can see with your natural eyes, there is a spiritual world, and it is the unseen things that last forever. Because of this, true greatness cannot be defined by status or accomplishments in this life. It must be defined by your impact in the next life.

True greatness does not begin with accomplishments. It begins with *relationship*. Jesus shared the secret of greatness when he said, "Now this is eternal life: that they *know you*, the only true God, and Jesus Christ, whom you have sent" (John 17:3 NIV).

Consider the implications of his message. Eternal life is a lot longer than the seventy or eighty years we get on this earth. Jesus just lit on fire our cultural idols of accomplishment and status. According to him, true greatness is relationship with God.

When you zoom out from the chaos of everyday life, this perspective makes perfect sense. In a thousand years, will anyone remember your invention, your hit song, or your successful business? What about in ten thousand years? If God is God and eternity is real, then a great life is one that is lived in authentic, growing relationship with him. To know God, I mean really know him—this is life itself!

But is a vibrant, personal relationship with God a real possibility? To know God … think about that! Not just to know about him or to know godly principles, but to actually operate daily from a living relationship with him. To hear his voice, to know his heart, and to exist in the center of his plan. This is the bull's-eye of what it means to live a truly great life!

The central message of the gospel is that relationship with God is available to us through the cross of Jesus Christ. He died for your sins, overcame death, and eternally removed the barrier between you and God. By faith in him, you can know God and live in the center of his will. This is what your heart has been looking for all along in the thirst for status and attention. Those things are imposters, preventing you from realizing what your heart really aches for—relationship with God. Nothing else will satisfy. And through his death and resurrection, Jesus makes that relationship a real possibility.

. . . .

Those things are imposters, preventing you from realizing what your heart really aches for—relationship with God. Nothing else will satisfy.

. . . .

So if the door is actually open, how do we run through it? How do we draw close to God and live a life in which the promises of Jesus become an experiential reality?

In his classic book *Good to Great*, Jim Collins tells the story of Dave Scott, winner of six Ironman Triathlons, and his habit of rinsing his cottage cheese before eating it.[6] Scott believed that the extra rinse would get excess fat off the cheese, sculpting his diet to the most minuscule detail. He wanted to win and reach his full potential so badly that no sacrifice was too great and no detail was too small.

Top-level athletes do things like this all the time, taking their training further and pushing themselves beyond where they've gone before. We hear about this type of dedication, and it doesn't surprise us. If you want to win six Ironman Triathlons, we understand that it's going to require that you embrace some uncommon habits. No one thinks Dave Scott is crazy for his behavior, because he is doing what it takes to win.

If God can really be known, and if a truly great life *is* relationship with him, then why doesn't our pursuit of him reflect this cottage-cheese-rinsing intensity? Why do uncommon habits often seem extreme and unrealistic for the follower of Jesus? When the apostle Paul taught the church in Corinth about living in real relationship with God, he used the analogy of an athlete.

> Do you not know that in a race all the runners run, but only one receives the prize? So run that you may obtain it. Every athlete exercises self-control in all things. They do it to receive a perishable wreath, *but we an imperishable.* (1 Corinthians 9:24–25)

How foolish does a perishable wreath look in comparison to knowing the Creator of the universe? And yet, Dave Scott—who is pursuing an earthly prize—is rinsing his cottage cheese, while many followers of Jesus—who are pursuing an imperishable prize—hesitate to embrace habits that disrupt any of our comforts. If Olympians can show this level of intensity, and all they obtain is a trophy or medal, then what about those who have been promised eternal life? What about those who have access to a real relationship with God and whose actions today have implications forever?

Maybe the missing element to a truly great life has less to do with God's willingness to move and more to do with our unwillingness to move. The greater life we yearn for is actually obtainable, but it's going to take a significant shift in our perspective and behavior to obtain it.

I remember the first time the weight of Jeremiah 29:13 settled on my soul. It's here that God plainly states what it will take to experience real relationship with him in this life: "You will seek Me and find Me when you search for Me with all your heart" (NASB). All your heart. That's what it takes. Half your heart doesn't get you there with God.

Imagine for a minute what your life would look like if this truth were applied, if you actually redirected your attention toward relationship with God as your *central goal in life*. How would life be different if your personal pursuit of him eclipsed your career ambitions, your desire for new comforts, your hobbies, your recreation—even your family and friends?

Does that sound extreme? Of course it does. But in light of the cross and the truth of eternity, it also sounds like the only practical way to live. Something deep on the inside calls out to you right now, even as you read these words, because you were created to do something great. Something *more*. You can't settle for a dull, distant, spiritual life.

The history books of heaven are full of people who took the words of Jesus seriously, and eternity has been shaped through their sacrifice. People like the apostle Paul, Martin Luther, Corrie ten Boom, William Seymour, Jim Elliot, and Dietrich Bonhoeffer. Normal people whose hearts were captured by an eternal purpose. Consider the perspective of Jonathan Edwards, one of history's greatest preachers:

> On the supposition, that there never was to be but one individual in the world, at any one time, who was properly a complete Christian, in all respects of a right stamp, having Christianity always shining in its

true luster, and appearing excellent and lovely, from whatever part and under whatever character viewed: Resolved, To act just as I would do, if I strove with all my might to be that one, who should live in my time.[7]

What an amazing ambition. Edwards was resolved to be the one person in his time who really walked with God. He wasn't waiting for someone else to do it. He took God's invitation seriously and responded with all his heart. But where are the followers of Jesus today who will pick up the baton that Edwards carried?

It's up to you and me. God's Spirit on the inside of us is calling. Will you settle for your current level of spiritual experience, or will you dive deeper? Will you respond to the call of God and even rearrange the way you live so that relationship with him becomes the central goal of your life?

I want to invite you to a funeral. It may sound a little strange, but sometimes a funeral is necessary. At this funeral, we will bury the old ordinary you—your ordinary life, ordinary faith, ordinary prayer, ordinary routines—and replace ordinary with something greater. It will require significant change, but the change is possible by God's Holy Spirit. Everything begins with you saying *yes*.

Jesus, I want a deeper relationship with you. Forgive me for accepting far less than you have made available. Right now, I say yes. Awaken my heart with a passion for you that goes beyond every other passion in my life. I choose to seek you with all my heart.

Chapter Two

HOW CHRISTIANS GROW

The importance of grace in spiritual growth

**"You then, my child, be strengthened by
the grace that is in Christ Jesus."**
2 Timothy 2:1

At age thirteen, during a church service in a large converted office building just outside the downtown area of the city, I had a life-altering encounter with God. My life can be best understood as falling into two parts: "before that moment" and "after that moment."

Before that moment, I was an altogether normal kid. I had no spiritual awareness or ambition that I can remember. I rarely attended church and had no interest in what God had to say. I wasn't searching for God. My life revolved around my friends, sports, and girls.

After that moment, the entire world looked different. It's hard to put into words the impact of the change, but from that time forward, I found within my heart an inexplicable hunger for God. Almost overnight, I started *caring*. I cared about what God thought, and I cared about what pleased him. More than anything else, I wanted to actually know him.

I started reading the Bible and praying, attending church every time the doors were open, and constantly asking God to align my life with his plan. But something strange was happening, and it wasn't long before the requirements of a godly life started piling up. Did I read the Bible enough? Did I devote enough time to prayer? Did I honor him today with my thoughts and my motives? Soon, all my attempts to live for Jesus were frustrated by my inability to perform. I tried to live holy, walk away from sin, and love others. I tried really hard. It just seemed that I wasn't very good at living like a Christian.

In the shopping plaza near my house growing up stood a huge bronze statue of Atlas holding up the world. In Greek mythology, Atlas was one of the Titans, condemned to hold up the weight of the world on his shoulders for eternity. I would ride my bike past the statue and couldn't help but stare at it as I passed by. I remember the strained look on Atlas's face with the massive weight of the planet resting on his shoulders. It isn't easy carrying that kind of weight every minute of every day.

Within my first year of trying to follow Jesus, I started looking and feeling more and more like Atlas. I felt like I didn't pray enough, or give enough, or love enough. My thoughts weren't holy, I'd keep running back to sin, and I'd find myself at the front of the church week after week confessing the same crimes to God. I would raise my hand at the end of the service to give my life to Jesus. Then I'd do it again the next week. After promising Jesus that I would do better, temptation would appear, and eventually I would crumble. Each week, the same routine. Each week, the same result.

A couple of years into this cycle, I found myself discouraged and exhausted. I remember shouting one day, "Jesus, how can I follow you if my sins are too strong for me to resist? If you aren't powerful enough to actually change me, then everything I believe about you is a lie!"

I had hit the wall. I just couldn't be *Christian* enough.

Maybe you've experienced some of this tension yourself, always feeling like you don't measure up to the requirements of God. The apostle Paul describes his internal battle when he writes, "I know that nothing good lives in me, that is, in my sinful nature. I want to do what is right, but I can't. I want to do what is good, but I don't. I don't want to do what is wrong, but I do it anyway" (Romans 7:18–19 NLT).

Paul tells us that the desire to obey is present, but the power to perform is not. He really *wants* to be a great man of God, but every time he tries, something on the inside interrupts his progress.

Most of us know this frustration firsthand. Have you ever tried to give up an addiction, walk away from a temptation, or say no to a destructive habit, only to find yourself back again, unable to stop? Maybe you've battled with drug abuse, gambling, or pornography and it's controlled your life. Or maybe your battle has been more subtle and subversive. It surfaces as an insatiable thirst for approval, a codependent need for a new relationship, or a constant desire to prove yourself to those around you. You might struggle with laziness—or maybe you can't stop yourself from working every minute of every day.

I have found that, as soon as any follower of Jesus decides to pursue holiness, they will soon be confronted with their own inability to live holy. And almost every time, we try to fix the problem ourselves through behavior modification: just try harder.

Dealing with Poop

When I was nineteen years old, I traveled to the Philippines with a mission team from the US. As we went from village to village, the first thing that grabbed my attention was the kindness we received from the people. Although often living in extreme poverty, our hosts were generous and hospitable. It took my breath away.

But that wasn't the only thing that took my breath away. The beauty of the scenery and the kindness of the people were frequently interrupted by the overwhelming smell that dominated many of the villages. The people in these particular villages didn't have toilets, which meant that everyone in town didn't *go* to the bathroom when they *went* to the bathroom—so the smell could not be flushed away.

Open defecation is a life-and-death problem for about a billion people worldwide. And life with no toilets leads to contaminated water, and contaminated water leads to sick people. The problem is so serious that the sanitary revolution is commonly considered the most significant medical milestone of the last two hundred years.

Before we arrived in these remote villages in the Philippines, the federal government had launched a massive initiative to install toilets in every hut and public area where the problem was the most urgent. For a little while, it seemed that the issue had been solved, but then something unexpected happened.

Word began to spread among the villagers that they could sell their newly installed toilets for a good amount of money and pocket the profits. Soon, every toilet in town was being ripped up and sold, and many people were buying TVs with the money! Tragically, disease continued to spread, babies continued to die, and the problem kept growing. Few in the villages made the connection between the toilet they'd sold and the sickness they suffered.

This is a real-life example of the limitations of behavior modification. The government had changed the outer environment of the villagers, but it had failed to change the inner narrative the villagers embraced. The government tried to change *behavior* without first changing *perspective*. The people in these villages were not willing to change their habits just because an official with a clipboard told them to poop in a toilet.

People don't change because they are told to or even because they want to. We don't change because we should. People usually change their behavior only after the story of what they *believe* has been rewritten.

. . . .

People usually change their behavior only after the story of what they *believe* has been rewritten.

. . . .

In his book *Atomic Habits*, James Clear outlined three layers of behavioral change. The first layer is changing your *outcomes*. This is where most Christians start. You experience the love of God, put your faith in Jesus, and now you want to be a better person. You want to be holy, kind, and good, so you try to change your outcomes. The next time a lustful image pops up on your computer screen, you promise to look away. The next time that annoying person at work passes your desk, you tell yourself to smile. This is behavior modification, and it produces some change, but not enough.

The second layer of behavioral change is changing your *process*. This means that you design a new way of doing things in order to stop the bad behavior before it happens. It's behavior modification 2.0. The government in the Philippines was attempting to do this by creating a complex sewer system that allowed villagers to flush their poop.

As a follower of Jesus, you might commit to going to church every week, sign up to serve with an outreach team, or install accountability software on your computer. By doing these things, you are changing your process. Implementing a new routine will produce some change, but changing your process isn't enough. Soon, you will find yourself working around your new process to get back to your old behavior.

So a third layer of behavioral change is necessary. James Clear called it changing your *identity*. He wrote, "Outcomes are about what you get. Processes are about what you do. Identity is about what you believe."[8]

If you really want to grow and become more like Christ, then you can't begin by trying to change your outcomes or trying to change your process. If you do, you will soon feel like Atlas holding the world on your shoulders and buckling under the pressure, because God never intended for you to carry that weight. His plan is not behavior modification through human effort but identity transformation by divine intervention. God must first change the core of your identity, then you must change the way you see things, and from this new perspective the power to actually change your behavior overflows.

The New Heart

To understand God's plan for spiritual growth, we must first sharpen our understanding of what Jesus actually came to accomplish. In John chapter 6, a great crowd surrounded Jesus and asked him their version of the age-old question: How do we live a life pleasing to God?

"Then they said to him, 'What must we *do*, to be *doing* the works of God?'" (John 6:28). Notice the emphasis of their question. It's all about doing. They wanted to know what they had to do to please God. They were trying to change their outcomes through self-effort.

The problem with this way of thinking is that it never leads to assurance before God. If you fail at obedience, you're haunted by shame. If you succeed at behavior modification, you are flooded with self-righteousness. Either way, after all your effort, the question still lingers: "God, did I do enough? How much is enough?"

It was at this point that Jesus gave the most counterintuitive answer to their question. "Jesus answered them, 'This is the work of God, that you *believe* in him whom he has sent'" (John 6:29).

I imagine that these people walked away scratching their heads, because the answer Jesus gave fights against everything that comes naturally to us. We think our acceptance comes from our doing. If you do good, you will be accepted. We must obey and perform. Then our acceptance is granted. Jesus, however, teaches that the greatest work you can *do* is to *believe*! Spiritual growth cannot begin with you changing your behavior. It must begin with a radical change in what you believe about God and about yourself!

Sandwiched within his lament about his inability to change, the apostle Paul teaches us God's secret for real spiritual growth: that beyond all human effort, God has acted on our behalf. Christ came to Earth in human form (Romans 3:25), lived the holy life that we could not (Romans 3:24), became our representative in heaven (Romans 6:23), and suffered the death that our sins deserved (Romans 5:6). He did this so that, by exchanging places with us, he would receive the judgment that belongs to us and we would receive the acceptance that belongs to him (Romans 5:17)! This is why we can shout with Paul,

"There is therefore now no condemnation for those who are in Christ Jesus" (Romans 8:1)!

Because of Christ, you are fully, forever forgiven by faith. Your sins are washed away, and you can freely receive the acceptance that belongs to Jesus!

Here we find the real secret of the gospel and the power for transformation. There is *now* no condemnation. That means right now. It's not just for later, once you're living in perfect holiness. It's for now. In the middle of your process of imperfection, you are already seen as perfect through the sacrifice of Christ! This is the one truth that changes everything else. God has acted on behalf of humanity, offering us *grace* through faith in the work of his Son.

The only way to obtain an assurance of God's acceptance is to abandon your philosophy of doing. Something else entirely must secure your position before God, and it cannot come from you. Theologians call this receiving an *alien righteousness*. That means that you must fully rely on the work of Christ rather than on your own works. This is the essence of grace: to receive freely what you don't deserve and cannot earn. The grace of God in Christ creates for the believer an atmosphere of acceptance. And it's this atmosphere that serves as a greenhouse for rich spiritual growth.

In their classic work *How People Grow*, Dr. Henry Cloud and Dr. John Townsend wrote that "when we finally understand that God isn't mad at us anymore, we become free to concentrate on love and growth instead of trying to appease him."[9] Did you catch that? Christ took all your sins on the cross and God has accepted the sacrifice; therefore, you can be sure that God isn't mad at you anymore! You no longer need to prove yourself to God—you just need to believe in his grace, and the atmosphere of acceptance produces the fruit of security.

. . . .

Christ took all your sins on the cross and God has accepted the sacrifice; therefore, you can be sure that God isn't mad at you anymore! You no longer need to prove yourself to God.

. . . .

You can let down your hair and take off your shoes. Rest in grace. You don't have to perform or justify yourself, and it's only in this environment that you can actually change and grow. Some wrongly assume that perfect acceptance from God would discourage the pursuit of holiness, but the opposite turns out to be true. A deep passion to pursue greater holiness grows from the revelation that God has pursued you and made you holy in Christ!

But the promise of the gospel does not end with the forgiveness of sin. Just as faith in the death of Jesus secures our forgiveness, so faith in the resurrection of Jesus initiates our transformation. God's Spirit takes up residence in our hearts and forges within us an unbreakable bond with himself. When we receive Christ, he removes the heart of stone and changes us at our core. Paul wrote, "But thanks be to God, that you who were once slaves of sin have become obedient *from the heart* to the standard of teaching to which you were committed" (Romans 6:17). This is a revolutionary truth: God has given every believer in Jesus *a new heart.*

In other words, the deepest part of you, the core of who you are, has been made new! It's been united with God and perfected in Christ. This is the promise spoken by the prophets (Ezekiel 36:26; Jeremiah 31:33) and fulfilled in Jesus!

Tragically, many Christians assume that their hearts are still wicked because the battle of sin continues to rage within them. God says, however, that though sin still seeks to conquer you, that is not who you truly are anymore. At your core, Christ has made your heart *good*. The prophet Jeremiah warned that the heart of man is desperately sick (Jeremiah 17:9), but Jesus has given you a new heart! Your new heart wants to follow and obey God, and the power of your obedience doesn't flow from self-effort; it flows from grace.

The ability to live a godly life comes from the inner revelation that you actually *are godly* through Christ. Before you can live as God requires, you must see yourself as God sees you. This is deeper than trying to change your outcomes (how you act) or trying to change your process (what you do). The death and resurrection of Jesus rewrite the inner narrative of your identity, and when you understand your God-given identity, you can live with God-given power.

True spiritual growth, then, seems to progress in a way exactly opposite to what we would expect. Our natural inclination is to try to learn the rules, do better, and form a sense of identity that is based on our good behavior. God, however, tells us to look to Jesus alone, receive his grace, discover acceptance in him, and form a new identity based on his love rather than on our own works.

It's not that God agrees with sin or that he takes sin lightly. Sin is as deadly as it ever was, and the death of Christ proves that. Sin can still destroy your life, and it will do so if you do not flee from it and learn to hate it; but it cannot be overcome through self-effort. It can only be overcome by faith in God's grace.

In other words, you can't work *for* acceptance, because if you do, you will never arrive. You must work *from* the acceptance that God has given freely through Jesus, leading to victory. And working from God's acceptance actually requires a deep denial of self because you must let go of your own self-righteousness. You must reject that inner compulsion to justify yourself through your own accomplishments. Paul called this the stumbling stone of grace because it's so easy to trip over. We want to justify ourselves and contribute to our own salvation. But in order for grace to be grace, it must be freely received.

Jesus explained this self-denial when he said, "If anyone would come after me, let him deny himself and take up his cross daily and follow me. For whoever would save his life will lose it, but whoever loses his life for my sake will save it" (Luke 9:23–24). The word used for "life" in this passage is not the Greek word *bios*, which describes the natural state of being alive, and it's not the Greek word *zoe*, which indicates the spiritual life-force that sustains all living things. Instead, Jesus intentionally used the word *psyche*, which refers to your inner, psychological life, or sense of self.

To follow Jesus, you must deny your old sense of self and let go of the identity that has been built on your good works. Dr. Timothy Keller wrote, "Your old way of having an identity, of gaining a sense of self, has got to end. In a sense, you have to die to it. And [Jesus] can give you a whole new identity. You'll get a whole new true self."[10]

Ultimately, coming to Jesus is not about giving up certain things or following certain rules but about letting go of your fractured, half-built sense of self and giving God center stage. No longer does your significance come from your accomplishments or your performance; it simply comes from God. He loves you, and he proved his love on the cross. In order for you to grow spiritually, you must choose to personally believe the truth that you are accepted in Christ. Real spiritual growth happens in the greenhouse of God's grace.

Theologian Thomas Chalmers put it this way:

> Seldom do any of our habits or flaws disappear by
> a process of extinction through reasoning or "by
> the mere force of mental determination." Reason
> and willpower are not enough. "But what cannot
> be destroyed may be dispossessed ... The only way
> to dispossess [the heart] of an old affection is by the
> expulsive power of a new one."[11]

What is the expulsive power that Chalmers speaks of? It's the love of God. As you believe in his love, it becomes the central force of your life and the core of your identity and worth. This is the secret of true spiritual growth: *grace makes you strong*.

When the apostle Paul taught his young protégé Timothy about spiritual growth, he said, "You then, my child, *be strengthened by the grace* that is in Christ Jesus, and what you have heard from me ... entrust to faithful men, who will be able to teach others also" (2 Timothy 2:1–2).

Notice the process that Paul emphasized in his instruction. Timothy was told to entrust the truths he had learned to others who could pass them on, but Paul specifically highlighted the truth that *grace makes you strong*! Not effort, not willpower, not natural ability, but grace.

Our hearts will try to convince us again and again that our performance leads to acceptance. In a way, performance does lead to acceptance, but it's Christ's performance on our behalf that, when received, produces assurance before God and the opportunity for real relationship.

But once we understand and accept his grace, how do we grow? How do we build a real relationship with God on the foundation of grace?

The Power of Pattern

In 1440, a middle-aged blacksmith named Johannes Gutenberg was fumbling around in his workshop with a world-shaping idea. Using the tools available, Gutenberg cobbled together a new invention—his first printing press. The mechanics were relatively simple. He used oil-based inks, a squeeze press, and durable metal type, setting the letters for each page in the appropriate places. Page by page, books were printed. Tedious work by our standards today, but lightning fast for that era, making obsolete the arduous scribbling of scribes and monks.

With Gutenberg's new invention, the cost of books plummeted across Europe, and literacy among the common people began to rise. Within sixty years, Gutenberg's creation would produce over 20 million volumes. Within one hundred years after that, the number would rise to over 200 million.[12] One man in his workshop had sparked a revolution, and the world would never be the same.

Because of Gutenberg, ideas and discoveries from around the globe were made widely available for the first time. Soon, new discoveries sprang up, standing on the shoulders of shared knowledge. The latest inventions, scientific research, philosophy of government, and biblical theology could all be read by the average person. It's incredible to think that the printing press ignited a reformation in religion, an enlightenment in culture, and an increase in the speed of scientific advancements—all because one man created a pattern.

Gutenberg himself did not generate any new knowledge. He was not a philosopher or a politician. The knowledge that propelled the transformation of culture was already available before Gutenberg's press. All he did was create a pattern, and the pattern unlocked unprecedented potential.

This illustration leads us to an intriguing idea. What if there were spiritual patterns that could unlock the explosive potential of God's grace? What if your greatest spiritual need was not more information or more opportunity, but simply a pattern that took what was already available and made it come alive?

This is a book about patterns. Together, we will study seven spiritual habits that create a pattern for explosive spiritual growth. These habits transcend culture, economic status, and ethnicity. They work in Milwaukee and in Hong Kong.

As you learn them, you may notice that there isn't anything particularly new about these habits. Their power and effectiveness are not found in their uniqueness; they're found in their synergy. Each habit builds upon the next. Each habit overlaps the previous ones and pushes you a little further. Together, these seven habits carry explosive spiritual power. Like Gutenberg's press, this simple pattern for spiritual growth can take what you already know and open up the floodgates of grace.

When God created the world, he built into the infrastructure of life the exponential power of pattern, forming all of life so that it would be reproduced using the system of a seed. Each plant carried within itself a seed that could reproduce after its own kind (Genesis 1:11). God didn't initially create every tree that would ever exist on the earth. Instead, he created a pattern that would continue to produce by itself. Sycamore trees produced more sycamore trees. Grizzly bears produced more grizzly bears. And, just like Gutenberg's printing press, the results were exponential. One seed can grow into a tree, and that tree can produce millions of seeds through its fruit.

The human brain was built for patterns. You learned patterns as a baby that helped you walk and talk. You learned patterns as a kid that taught you how to deal with a bully or to write with a pencil. You learned patterns as an adult that taught you how to handle money, success, and failure. Psychologist Albert Bandura wrote, "Most human behavior is learned observationally through modeling: from observing others, one forms an idea of how new behaviors are performed, and on later occasions this coded information serves as a guide for action."[13] The truth is that you've been subconsciously collecting patterns your entire life.

I grew up watching Michael Jordan play basketball in the 1990s. I bought his sneakers, rooted for his team, and followed every stat of his career. One day while I was playing basketball with some friends, I caught myself sticking out my tongue as I drove to the basket. Why would I do that? Without realizing it, I had internalized one of Michael Jordan's signature quirks. Somewhere in my subconscious, my brain had programmed my tongue to stick out of my mouth every time I tried to get to the rim like MJ. If only my brain were strong enough to get my legs to jump like his could!

Patterns enter our minds in seed form, often small and unnoticed, and then begin to create a standard for how we think. Over time, the patterns we embrace form a framework. They influence the way we dress, the way we talk, and the food we eat. Nearly every element of your day has been dramatically shaped by the patterns you've learned, and many of them are good.

But some of these patterns are the hidden source of your problems, because the pattern you internalize eventually becomes the *normal* that you accept. Maybe in your house when you were a kid it was normal to lie. Or maybe it was normal to never talk about your feelings. Maybe it was normal to watch TV seven hours a day.

This is where the power of pattern can work against us, because far too often we've embraced a *normal* that is far from God's best. The patterns we've adopted produce a Christianity that doesn't resemble God's model, and with the loss of the pattern many times comes the loss of the blessing. Soon, God's amazing promises for things like perfect peace (Philippians 4:7) and strength to overcome (1 John 4:4) sound more like wishful thinking than obtainable reality.

But the breakdown is not with God! That's why Paul warns us, "Do not conform to the *pattern* of this world, but be transformed by the *renewing* of your mind" (Romans 12:2 NIV).

Imagine your mind as a map showing roads and highways. These roads have been paved by years of thinking. For many of us, our thoughts about God and our own identities have been misinformed, creating within us skinny dirt roads, full of dark corners and steep cliffs. We aren't sure what God is like or what he'll do. Sometimes he feels close, and other times we're convinced that he's forgotten us. This foggy, unpaved way of thinking about God leads to slow, difficult progress in our spiritual growth.

Through faith in Christ, God removes your heart of stone and gives you a new heart. As you renew your mind with this truth, the skinny dirt roads in your thinking are replaced with the smooth, wide highways of grace. No longer are you rejected; in Christ, you are accepted. No longer are you condemned; now, you are forgiven. No longer are you broken; now, you are healed. No longer are you distant; now, you are close. As your faith takes hold of God's promises, God renews your perspective, and the crooked roads of your mind are transformed into a superhighway, where God's grace can travel unhindered.

This doesn't mean that spiritual maturity will be realized overnight. Much of our spiritual growth takes a lifetime. But it does mean that the work of God in your life will speed up and your spiritual progress can start being tracked in miles rather than inches.

Build Me a Highway

Years ago, on a trip to Germany, a friend handed me the keys to his Volkswagen and said, "Let's take a ride." He led me out onto the Autobahn, the German highway without speed limits, and told me that I could go as fast as I wanted.

As an American, this was a completely foreign concept. I had never traveled on a road without a speed limit. Something inside of me came alive as I fulfilled every young boy's dream and pressed the accelerator to the floor. We flew that day, going faster than I'd ever moved in a car, and I'll never forget the feeling.

In the chapters that follow, we will travel together through seven specific habits that form a lifestyle of unprecedented spiritual growth. Some of the habits will come easily. Others will require a complete restructuring of your life. But there is something inside all of us that longs to reach new speeds on the road of spiritual growth, and these habits can become for us a highway with limitless potential.

But before we can learn these habits, we need to find the on-ramp of the highway. Paul gives us a framework for thinking that prepares our hearts for spiritual growth:

> But when the goodness and loving kindness of God our Savior appeared, he saved us, not because of works done by us in righteousness, but according to his own mercy, by the washing of regeneration and renewal of the Holy Spirit, whom he poured out on us richly through Jesus Christ our Savior, so that being justified by his grace we might become heirs according to the hope of eternal life. (Titus 3:4–7)

These four verses contain four important truths that must be deeply internalized if we are to travel the Autobahn of growth in grace.

Truth #1: God Is for You. Paul begins by telling us that the goodness of God has *appeared*. Now, God didn't change—he's always been good. But through Jesus, God's goodness has been made obvious and indisputable.

The cross is the irrefutable evidence of his goodness. In a court of law, circumstantial evidence rarely holds up. In the same way, if you build your perspective of God on your circumstances, your faith won't hold up through the challenges of life. But we've got DNA evidence. His blood was shed at the scene. This evidence is stronger than our feelings and our circumstances.

Jesus proved that God is *for you*. He has a good plan for your life, and he is working even bad things for your eventual good (Romans 8:28). If you will believe this, it's like putting your car into first gear. Now you can begin to move.

Truth #2: You Exist for Him. After Paul tells us about God's goodness, he states that God has saved us, not because of works done by us, but according to *his own mercy*. This is important: we did not save ourselves. God didn't save you because you were worthy. Rather, he saved you *just because*. Because he's God. Because he can. Most importantly, because of love! When you sit back and let this truth sink in, it does something profound on the inside. God *chose* you. Why did he open your eyes and draw your heart to himself? It's a mystery. The only answer he gives is that he chose you because he loves you (Deuteronomy 7:7–8).

God chose you, which means you belong to him and you exist for him. You serve his story, not the other way around. He gets to be God and you get to be his child. Since truth #1 is that God is for you, you don't have to be scared of existing for him. His glory and your good run on parallel tracks! God has proven through the cross that he is for you, and this confidence allows you to live unreservedly for him. Existing for God satisfies your ache to be great, since you're walking with your Creator. But at the same time, it suffocates your thirst for the spotlight, because you're serving his story rather than your own. Existing for him offers your heart perfect freedom as you rest in his goodness and entrust your dreams into his capable hands.

Truth #3: You Haven't Reached Your Max. Paul then adds that we were saved by the washing of regeneration and renewal of the Holy Spirit, whom God poured out on us richly through Jesus Christ. The Holy Spirit now lives within you, and it's critical to notice the degree to which the Spirit has been given. Paul tells us that the Spirit has been poured out richly!

The word *richly* is a word used to describe wealthy people—those with a super-abundance that overflows on every side. God, who has no shortage of power, has *richly* poured his power into you, and his Holy Spirit in you causes a fundamental change in your capacity. You now have a reservoir of divinity abiding in your soul, which means that your potential is limitless. There is more available—more peace, more miracles, more life! If God is in your heart, then there's more in your tank!

Truth #4: Eternity Reframes Everything. Paul concludes with the statement "So that being justified by his grace we might become heirs according to the hope of eternal life." The word *heirs* speaks of family. Since the Spirit of Christ lives in you, the inheritance of Christ will be given to you. But this is more than natural family; this is forever family, because we have the hope of eternal life! For our finite minds, this idea is so difficult to grasp, but if we can catch a glimpse of eternity, the problems of today will instantly begin to shrink.

Now that you are convinced that God is for you, aware that you exist for him, trusting God for greater capacity, and leaning into his eternal purpose, your heart is ready to grow.

Reaching Your Full Potential

Gymnast Gabby Douglas moved a thousand miles away from home at age fourteen to train for the Olympics. She spent all day, every day, working in a gym with people she hardly knew, far from her family, her friends, and any semblance of a normal life so that she could compete at the highest level. She went on to win gold medals, but behind the story of her success is a much longer story of sacrifice and discipline. She had committed herself to life-altering habits. There was simply no other way.

In his instructions to Timothy, Paul explained how not all followers of Jesus reach their full potential:

> Now in a great house there are not only vessels of gold and silver but also of wood and clay, some for honorable use, some for dishonorable. Therefore, if anyone cleanses himself from what is dishonorable, he will be a vessel for honorable use, set apart as holy, useful to the master of the house, ready for every good work. (2 Timothy 2:20–21)

Did you notice what separates the vessel of gold from the vessel of clay? Paul tells us that it isn't a predetermined fate. Instead, he says that if *anyone* cleanses himself, he will be a vessel of honor. What can that mean except that greatness in God's kingdom is open to anyone! We can't grow by self-effort or conquer sin by trying harder, but we can step forward in faith. We can actively receive the grace of God and begin to develop habits that will allow his grace within us to grow.

For the last twenty years, I've tested and experimented with various personal disciplines in my pursuit of God. I've learned from dozens of mentors and teachers, and over time, seven key habits have emerged. These are the habits that have been most beneficial in my own life, and as I've shared them with others, I have been amazed by the miraculous impact they have had.

The seven habits can be broken down into three function categories. The first three habits I call *Finding Your Center*. They are intended to help you reframe all of life around a relationship with God. Habits four and five are what I call *Guard Rail Habits*. They will help you keep your spiritual life from flying off the tracks. I've put habits six and seven under the category *Long Haul Living*. They will help you to stay the course year after year and decade after decade.

It's important to note that I don't believe that these seven habits encompass the totality of the Christian life. Not even close. There are hundreds of other personal disciplines that are incredibly beneficial for Christian maturity. At its core, Christianity is far more than habits, and God can never be fit in to our programs.

One more thing: you will never actually finish this book. You may finish reading it, but you won't ever *arrive*, at least not in this life. I've learned that, as soon as I feel healthy and strong in one or two of the habits, a brief survey of the others will reveal how much attention they need. I've never met anyone who is operating at an optimal level in all seven habits. At least one always seems to require immediate attention.

But don't let that discourage you. The goal is not to master these habits but to reach God. These habits serve as a catalyst to push your heart closer and closer to him. And with God, the closer you get, the more you can see the depth of what he's made available. Like drawing water from a bottomless well, we will never reach the end of his love.

Father God, right now I open my heart to a new way of living. I want to begin to create new patterns that draw me closer to you. Prepare my heart. Set me on fire with a deeper passion to know you. I move toward you in faith.

PART 2: FINDING YOUR CENTER

"I have had more trouble with D. L. Moody than with any other man."[14]

D. L. Moody

"When God gets relegated to second place behind any bauble or trinket, I have swapped the pearl of great price for painted fragments of glass."[15]

Brennan Manning

"I am attempting to rest in alert availability."[16]

Alicia Britt Chole

 Chapter Three

THE HABIT OF RELATIONSHIP

Spending time alone with God regularly

"And rising very early in the morning, while it was still dark, he departed and went out to a desolate place, and there he prayed."

Mark 1:35

For years, I've been trying to shake it. I've definitely gotten better, but in full transparency I must admit that, for as long as I can remember, I have had the propensity to be a hurrier. I try to squeeze too many things into one day. I underestimate the time things will take or overestimate my efficiency. The other day, for example, I was heating up a cup of coffee in the microwave. I was by myself, and I stood there watching the seconds tick away on the little screen until I caught myself talking out loud. "Come on, come on …"

I was talking to a microwave. As if speaking to it would make it work any faster.

I catch myself doing the same thing in elevators. Right after I push the floor-number button, my hand is drawn to the door-close button.

And I can't press it once. I have to hold it—or even better, press it twenty times. Door close, door close, door close. "Come on, come on …" It's not that I necessarily need to get to where I'm going faster; it's just that I like to save the 1.2 seconds it takes for the door to close.

What is wrong with me?

Psychologists call this *hurry sickness*, and I'm pretty sure I'm not the only one suffering from this disease. It's defined by experts as a need to move faster even when life does not require it.

I recently read an article that disclosed a little secret of the elevator-manufacturing companies. Often, the door-close button is connected only to a light bulb![17] It doesn't actually close the door any faster, but research has found that having the button serves as a mechanical placebo for all the ridiculous people who feel the need to hit that button twenty times to save the extra 1.2 seconds. Apparently, all my hurrying, all that button-pushing, isn't actually getting me anywhere faster.

A few weeks before I wrote this chapter, my wife and I wanted to watch a movie with our three sons, and we eventually landed on the old 1990s movie *Twister*. As you may recall, *Twister* is about a group of scientists who chase tornadoes to better understand the storms and provide earlier warning for storm-prone areas. The movie is action packed, but the essence of the plot can be summed up rather succinctly: chase a tornado, chase a tornado, chase a tornado … catch the tornado … run! Run from the tornado, run from the tornado, run from the tornado!

For 1 hour and 53 minutes, I watched my boys sit on the edge of their seats and couldn't help but think, *Is this not an accurate picture of our lives?* I feel like I spend so much of my energy either chasing a tornado or running from a tornado. We're chasing the kids, chasing the career, chasing the promotion, chasing the diploma; then we're running from that difficult conversation, avoiding that family member, not making eye contact with the boss … running from the tornado.

This kind of life reveals a problem that goes a lot deeper than elevator delays or cold cups of coffee. Our hurry on the outside is evidence of a bigger issue on the inside.

Very rarely do we make room for deep thought, honest reflection, personal assessment, or inner pause. Staying busy has become for many of us a defense mechanism to keep us from ever facing the deeper questions of life. Why am I really here? What am I supposed to do with the time I have? What do I actually believe about eternity, and how should that change the way I live?

. . . .

Staying busy has become for many of us a defense mechanism to keep us from ever facing the deeper questions of life.

. . . .

Rather than thinking deeply about these things, we distract ourselves with TV or music or social media, always keeping ourselves entertained enough to never inwardly engage.

Too often, the distance we feel toward God has nothing to do with him. He has been knocking on our door, waiting there for us, but the noise on the inside is so loud that we can't hear his voice.

Imagine trying to build a deep relationship with a friend, but every time you're together, the radio is turned all the way up. Imagine trying to write down directions to a destination while standing in the middle of a marching band as they play their opening song. For many of us, these are accurate pictures of our interior lives. Until we stop chasing the tornado, deep relationship with God is impossible.

A Seeking-God Lifestyle

When I was a new Christian, someone introduced me to the idea of *quiet time*. The name sounded to me like something you do with a three-year-old after a long day at preschool. By quiet time, my friend meant a time of your day, free from distraction, specifically devoted to prayer and Bible reading. Some call it "daily devotions" or "time with God." It's not that the rest of your day is time without God, but this specific time is focused, planned, and set aside.

As a new follower of Jesus, I decided that this would become a part of my routine, so I set out to devote time every morning for prayer and Bible reading. I had a small group of friends who agreed to do this with me, and it didn't take long before we found ourselves running into some challenges. Maybe you can relate.

First, I got tangled up in the guilt game. If I didn't pray and read the Bible on a particular day, my confidence before God would evaporate. As soon as I committed to having daily time with God, my mind turned this commitment into a law, and I believed that my relationship with God was on the line if I didn't follow through. Did I pray enough today? Did I read enough today? Did I do enough to be sure that he would answer my prayers? Insecure thoughts like these will complicate any relationship.

My friends and I decided to challenge one another by setting up an accountability group. The agreement was that, if one of us missed our daily time with God, that person would pay twenty dollars to one of the other guys. Soon, our gatherings started to look more like horse betting than Jesus loving, as money was exchanged back and forth and people argued about what "missing our time" really meant.

It's amazing how your mind can justify things when money is on the line. I'd think things like, *Well, I sort of prayed for a bit during that thirty-minute drive yesterday, so that counts toward my time with God. I don't have to say I missed yesterday.* Unfortunately, we weren't just missing our time with God … we were missing the point.

And even when we did actually devote uninterrupted time to seeking God, each of us faced the same seemingly insurmountable hurdle: quieting our thoughts. I would last about five minutes before I started watching the squirrels out the window. My mind would wander in a thousand directions. I legitimately remember times when I forgot the reason I was sitting alone in my room. What was I supposed to be doing? Oh yeah, praying. In a world of nonstop entertainment and distractions, learning to sit still and talk to God doesn't come easily. Listening and waiting for him to speak are even harder. This was going to take some practice.

Above all, the biggest mistake we made in our daily time with God had to do with the motive behind the habit. We were more focused on getting something done or checking a box. Somewhere along the line, we had completely missed the central point, which was to seek God.

Relationship with God is not about doing something for God or getting things from God, but about *getting God himself.* The Christian faith is built on the truth that God is not just the one who answers your deepest needs. He himself *is* your deepest need. Life is less about knowing what to do and more about knowing him!

A. W. Tozer wrote, "What comes into our minds when we think about God is the most important thing about us."[18] If this is true, and I believe it is, then the biggest problem in your life is not your finances, your job, your health, or your relationships. Your biggest problem is an inaccurate view of God. The great purpose behind prayer and Bible reading is to invite God to reshape the vision of himself in your heart.

We don't see him clearly, not as clearly as he wants to be seen. And until that changes, our hearts can't grow. Although God is unchanging and always consistent, this doesn't mean that he is simple. His ways are higher than our ways, and to recognize God in the midst of the chaos of life, we must become progressively more acquainted with his complexities through an ever-deepening investment in relationship.

A few years ago, I spent a week away from my family on a ministry trip. My son Noah was two years old at the time, and his normal routine when I came home from work was to rush to the front door as soon as he heard my car. Every day I came home, it was as if Santa Claus had just arrived. I would open the door and he would jump into my arms without a second's hesitation. I'd scoop him up and give him a kiss, and then he'd shuffle away to play with his toys.

On this particular day, I expected an even more exuberant welcome since I had been away for a week. I could already hear his little feet pounding toward the entrance as I approached the house. I swung open the door and reached out my arms, but rather than diving into my chest, Noah looked at me, stopped dead in his tracks, then ran to my wife. What was wrong?

That week, I hadn't shaved and my beard had grown in. When the door opened, Noah didn't recognize me. I looked like a stranger to my son!

For many of us, God's work in our lives is misunderstood or misinterpreted because we haven't learned to recognize him in the different seasons of life. We become comfortable with a clean-shaven God who answers prayers and gives us peace. But how does God look in the midst of a storm? How does he look in the midst of loss?

Tragically, many invitations from God go ignored or rejected because people opened the door and saw only a stranger. Learning to recognize God in the various ways that he speaks and moves takes time. Unfortunately, most Christians devote only a few minutes at best each day to seek God. The result is an underdeveloped, immature understanding of who he is.

No one learns trigonometry in ten minutes. How can we expect to develop an accurate view of the Creator of the universe with a couple of minutes of prayer before we hustle off to work?

. . . .

How can we expect to develop an accurate view of the Creator of the universe with a couple of minutes of prayer before we hustle off to work?

. . . .

The challenge with knowing God is that he is not like anyone else you know. This is what the Scripture means when it teaches that God is *holy*. He is set apart. He's different from everyone else in the world. To actually know him, you must intentionally and methodically reprogram your thoughts about him. Your natural thinking must be replaced with supernatural thinking. As you begin to see God for who he really is, your view of him creates a lens through which all of life can be understood. An accurate view of God leads to exponential spiritual growth.

Paul expressed this thought when he wrote, "And we all, with unveiled face, beholding the glory of the Lord, are being transformed into the same image from one degree of glory to another" (2 Corinthians 3:18).

Making time for *beholding* God is the key to becoming more like him. And the more like him you become, the more joy, power, love, and peace you will experience. The more clearly you see God, the more accurately you will see yourself and the world around you. Developing an accurate view of God is the foundation of all spiritual growth.

In order to approach God, we must first internalize the truth that he is approachable. When we first learn to pray, many of us tend to approach God hesitantly. We often feel unworthy, like we don't know how to do it right. That's why renewing our minds with God's truth is so important. It provides the framework for real relationship.

Jesus teaches us that before God becomes our judge, ruler, or king, God's first relationship to us is as our *father*. "This, then, is *how* you should pray: 'Our *Father* in heaven, hallowed be your name'" (Matthew 6:9 NIV).

Have you personally learned to approach God as Father? How would your prayers look different if you were deeply convinced of the father-heart of God?

After struggling through the first few months of trying to have daily time with God, something started to shift in my heart. My friends and I decided to stop charging each other twenty dollars when we missed our times of prayer. God began speaking to me through the Scripture, revealing to my heart that he wanted a Father-son relationship.

At first, this felt foreign and unnatural. I can't casually talk to God! But the more I read about the life of Jesus and the more I understood the gospel, the more precious this opportunity became. God wants to meet with me every day. He wants to teach me his secrets and unveil his truth. He wants to guide me, carry me, comfort me, and train me. And he wants the same for you.

Years ago, I came across an old hymn by C. Austin Miles. It's called "In the Garden":

I come to the garden alone,
While the dew is still on the roses,
And the voice I hear, falling on my ear,
The Son of God discloses.

He speaks, and the sound of His voice
Is so sweet the birds hush their singing;
And the melody that He gave to me
Within my heart is ringing.

I'd stay in the garden with Him
Tho' the night around me be falling;
But He bids me go; thro' the voice of woe,
His voice to me is calling.

And He walks with me, and He talks with me,
And He tells me I am His own,
And the joy we share as we tarry there,
None other has ever known.[19]

I love the way the author describes intimacy with God. He makes it clear that it's possible. It's available. God wants to share his deepest secrets with you. He wants to become your confidant and closest companion. He wants to *father* you. God is calling you right now to a deeper level of relationship, but you have to answer the call.

See You in the Morning

The gospel of Mark records a story about when Jesus spent an entire evening praying for the sick and demon-possessed, and the whole city came out to see him. After this long, exhausting night, Mark tells us what Jesus did the following morning: "And rising very early in the morning, while it was still dark, he departed and went out to a desolate place, and there he prayed" (Mark 1:35).

This isn't the only time we read of Jesus doing this. In fact, the gospel accounts make it clear that disappearing in the morning was his regular routine. After a long night of exhausting ministry, Jesus didn't veg out or sleep in. Instead, he got up very early, while it was still dark, and met with his Father *alone*.

Why did he do this first thing in the morning after such a tiring night? Couldn't he have slept a little longer, checked Instagram, answered some emails, and then taken time for prayer and reflection?

In the Old Testament, there is a story about the people of Israel in the wilderness when God provided manna, a sort of bread from heaven that fell every morning from the sky. The people only had to go outside and pick it up off the ground and they could eat it. They were told to take only what they needed for the day, because any manna left over on the next morning would rot. By the time the morning was over, the manna was gone. "Morning by morning they gathered it, each as much as he could eat; but when the sun grew hot, it melted" (Exodus 16:21).

The manna is a picture of our spiritual lives. Our spirits need to feast on God to grow, but when we put exercise, social media, or email ahead of time with him, we will often find ourselves more distracted and less spiritually productive. The manna melted because we didn't seek God first.

What I call *the principle of the first* can be seen throughout the stories of Scripture. Whatever you do first has huge implications for the rest of what you will do (Matthew 6:33). Making time for God first thing in the morning is an expression of your priorities. It's a way to tell God with your actions that he is first in your life.

Abraham rose first thing in the morning on the day he trusted God with his son, and his faith was proven. Moses received the Ten Commandments first thing in the morning. Joshua was given instruction from God for the great battle of Jericho first thing in the morning. Gideon received his call from God to deliver the nation first thing in the morning. Are you recognizing a pattern?

I believe that God has placed a unique power in the morning. There is no other time quite like it. King David understood this truth when he wrote, "In the morning, LORD, you hear my voice; in the morning I lay my requests before you and wait expectantly" (Psalm 5:3 NIV). David was expectant because he believed in a God who answered prayer and because he was seeking God first thing—before seeking anything or anyone else.

It's not that God won't answer your prayers in the middle of the day or that it does you no good to pray in the evening. Every time for prayer is a good time. But there is a certain magic to the morning. There is a power in seeking God first, above all else. Jesus understood this and modeled it for us.

We are told that when Jesus rose early to seek God, he *departed* and went to a *desolate place*. This was a place where other people couldn't find him, that only he and his Father knew about. I remember when I was in college and living with four roommates in one dorm room. I would wake up in the morning, but privacy was virtually impossible, so I began to scour the building for a desolate place. Finally, I found a small bathroom (yeah, I was desperate) on the basement level of my dorm. I would drag a chair into the bathroom, use the sink as my desk, and meet with God in that bathroom every morning.

And those times were *powerful*. It wasn't glamorous, and every once in a while, a hungover college student would stumble in and see me praying with my Bible open at the sink! Luckily, only rarely would they remember the incident. I learned in that season that making the extra effort to really be alone with God paid huge dividends. He is waiting to reveal himself, but in order to find him, you must pull away to a desolate place.

From Everyone to What's Next

Jesus got up early and found his desolate place, but eventually his disciples tracked him down and interrupted him. The conversation between Jesus and Peter reveals a powerful truth about daily time with God: "And Simon and those who were with him searched for him, and they found him and said to him, '*Everyone* is looking for you.' And he said to them, 'Let us go on to the *next* towns, that I may preach there also, for that is why I came out'" (Mark 1:36–38).

Peter illustrated for us the mind-set of the person who hasn't sought God first thing in the morning. Maybe he woke up late that day, still groggy from the night before. After slamming down some breakfast, he started hearing about how Jesus was missing. Soon, his mind became flooded with the concerns of *everyone*. What was everyone saying? What was everyone thinking? He rushed into his day, unaware of the fact that he was being driven by the pressures of what everyone else was thinking.

I've found that this is the default mind-set I slip into if I don't have time alone with God first. An unhealthy need for approval, a propensity to compare myself with others—it all comes so naturally unless I set the course of my day with God first thing in the morning.

When Peter finally found Jesus, he quickly expressed his urgent concerns. But Jesus didn't directly address them. Jesus strategically ignored Peter's frantic request … because he had been meeting with the Father. He had spent his morning in the desolate place, and his heart was centered and in step with God. Instead of being obsessed with the concerns of *everyone*, Jesus could clearly see *what was next*. This is the difference that meeting with God in the morning can make.

As a pastor, the number-one concern people in our church have presented to me over the years is their uncertainty about what's next. Discerning God's direction for your life can feel overwhelming. Does God want you to take this job or that one? Does he want you to go here or there? It seems that many followers of Christ feel crippled, wanting to know what God has next, but unsure of how to discern his plan.

When we seek God first, morning after morning, the deafening voices of "everyone" get quieter and the direction of God for the future gets clearer. It's in this time that God filters through your motives, reveals his purposes, and convinces your heart of his good intentions.

All deep relationships require uninterrupted time spent together, and relationship with God is no exception. Many followers of Jesus expect to grow spiritually with five minutes a day of prayer and a three-sentence devotional, and then they wonder why God feels distant and his direction seems unclear. Jesus models for us a life in step with the Father. Those who want to find God must find *time*.

How much time is enough? How much time should we actually set aside first thing in the morning? To answer this question, we must first decide our ultimate goal. Are we setting time aside in the morning just to survive spiritually? Is the goal to minimize stress or just not crumble under the pressures of life? Are we punching a clock to satisfy a religious obligation? Maintenance and survival cannot be the driving motivations behind time with God, and neither can duty. God himself must be our deepest motivation. We must want to know him!

When the value of knowing God eclipses every other desire, it's only a matter of time before your life is flooded with his presence.

In his book *Outliers*, Malcolm Gladwell popularized what he called the "Ten Thousand Hour Rule." He quoted neurologist Daniel Levitin, who wrote that

> ten thousand hours of practice is required to achieve the level of mastery associated with being a world-class expert—in anything ... In study after study, of composers, basketball players, fiction writers ... this number comes up again and again.... It seems that it takes the brain this long to assimilate all that it needs to know to achieve true mastery.[20]

People have debated this study since it came out, but it teaches us something powerful about how our brains are wired. For an activity to become second nature, it must be repeated for thousands of hours. In our context, if we are going to reframe our thinking about God, which shapes the way we see all of life, then the human mind will require hours of reprogramming.

It's one thing to read a Bible verse that tells you that God loves you, but it's a very different thing to live every moment of your day resting and abiding in his love. Which one do you want? If you want the truth of the gospel to become the window through which you view the world, what will it take?

The answer is *time*. Time meditating on his truth, listening for his voice, and learning to quiet your busy mind. If you spent one hour every morning alone with God, it would take 27.39 years to hit ten thousand hours.

One hour every morning—that will definitely mess up your routine. I've found that one hour alone with God is a helpful goal for a number of reasons. For one thing, it's long enough that it will completely disrupt your life. There is no way to just *squeeze* in an hour every morning. You have to plan for it, cancel other things for it, and go to bed earlier for it. It will be disruptive, and that's sort of the point. It is a declaration to God that he is your greatest priority.

One hour with God is also short enough to actually be possible. Most of us have to go to work or class or somewhere else in the morning, so spending more than an hour alone with God is usually unsustainable. Sixty minutes is long enough to really take ground spiritually but short enough to actually accomplish—with some significant sacrifice.

What if you tried this for the next thirty days? What if you rearranged your morning routine and put God first, before and above everything else? What could happen—in your relationships, in your career, in your own soul—if you took this challenge to draw near to God? How different would your life be if you lived every moment with a vibrant awareness of God? How different would your life be if his direction for your future came clearly into view? This one change in your routine is the front door to an entirely new way of living. It's the first of our seven habits.

Habit 1: *Spend the first hour of your*
morning alone with God.

If spending time in the morning alone with God is a completely new discipline for you, then this habit is going to take some time to develop. I remember how hard it was for me to focus during my time with God when I first started. I'd last five minutes before my mind had wandered off into some random distraction. Truthfully, in the early days I thought it was hopeless. But day after day, morning after morning, my spiritual capacity stretched.

If one hour seems overwhelming, start with fifteen minutes. Do that every day for a month. In month two, move to thirty minutes. Month three, try forty-five minutes. By month four, there's a good chance you will be ready for an hour with God.

If spending daily time with God is something you have done for years, let me challenge you on this point. After talking with hundreds of Christians about this topic, I've discovered that most followers of Jesus claim to spend daily time seeking God, but if we did an honest evaluation of our actual practice, the time we spend is minuscule.

Some people pray on their way in to work. Some people read a quick devotional before getting out of bed. Some listen to a sermon while they exercise. None of this is wrong, but these examples are not what I'm proposing. One hour of dedicated time, first thing every morning, will hurt. But it will open up a great spiritual door, and life will never be the same.

The principles we've covered so far shouldn't be legalistically enforced. Maybe you work nights. Maybe you have a newborn who is up at 4:00 a.m. Life is going to require some flexibility, but don't use that as an excuse to make your pursuit of God a low priority. Begin somewhere, and then grow from there. Where do you need to grow? Where have you gotten lazy? Do you need to overhaul your prayer life or approach the Scripture from a new angle?

Once you've decided to prioritize a seeking-God lifestyle, it's time to develop an intentional plan.

Planning Your Time with God

What do we actually do during our morning hour of seeking God? How do we fill that time to maximize its effectiveness for spiritual growth?

When I started out, I had no idea what to do, so I approached the Bible as if it were a textbook, beginning in Genesis and working my way through it. By the time I had gotten to Leviticus, I was losing my mind. Knowing where to start in the Bible and easing yourself into extended times of prayer will help, but this will be difficult sometimes. Prepare yourself for the challenge by actively believing that if you will just draw near to God, he promises to respond by drawing near to you (James 4:8).

A daily routine of seeking God can include a number of different practices and spiritual tools, but it's best to begin with the two most important elements. God uses the *Scripture* to restructure our minds with his truth and change the way we think, and he uses *prayer* to connect our hearts with his and advance his will on the earth. These two spiritual tools are like a fork and a knife: they work best when they're used together.

Just like stretching is a good idea before a workout, doing some preparation before coming to the Bible might be good as well. I find that my heart and mind are a little foggy early in the morning. So the first thing I do is find a place. Somewhere quiet and desolate. Through the years, the place has changed—from a dorm bathroom, to an attic, to my home office.

Once I'm alone, I'll often begin by reading a psalm. Sometimes I'll set an alarm and allow three to five minutes of silence to pass after I've read the psalm. This is my time to center. I'm careful not to open my email or check social media, which will quickly pull me into the world of *everyone*. This time belongs to God. Once my attention is set on God, I'm ready to engage. There are innumerable ways to pray and read the Scripture, but let's start with some foundational practices.

The Scripture

Approaching the Bible can be a little intimidating, especially if this is new for you. Here are three ways to study Scripture that I have found most helpful in my morning time. These practices will help you *SOW* God's truth deep into your heart: systematic reading, one-topic study, and waiting and repeating.

S—Systematic Reading: Choose one book in the Bible and read a portion of it each day until you've completed that book. Read it slowly. I recommend reading one or two chapters a day at the most. This will force you to chew on what you read. You'll be not just processing information but learning to hear God's Spirit and receive revelation.

If you are new to the Bible, I'd recommend beginning with the gospel of Mark. Then read the book of Acts, then Ephesians. Once you've worked your way through those, complete the rest of the New Testament. After that, begin on your way through the Old Testament.

As you read your chapter for the day slowly, pause over anything that grabs your attention. Try to become aware of the inner voice of the Holy Spirit. Stop throughout your reading and ask yourself: What stood out to me? What statement or phrase seemed to *shimmer*? Write these things down in a notebook that you always bring to your morning time with God, and try to put into words what it seems God is teaching you. What does this chapter reveal about God? What does this chapter reveal about life?

Once you've written down and reflected on anything that stood out, answer the question: What am I supposed to do with this? What application does this truth require? Try to be as specific as possible with your answer. If you are setting aside an hour with God, then this process can take anywhere from fifteen to forty-five minutes. It's one important way that you can begin to engage the Scripture.

O—One-Topic Study: A second way to approach the Bible is through a one-topic study. For example, in the back of most Bibles is a concordance that lists important words. Also, there are multiple websites where you can search for a keyword or phrase in Scripture. (Try biblegateway.com to start.) You could search "in Christ" and isolate every time in Scripture this phrase is used. You could search "Holy Spirit" or "peace."

Print out the results and slowly read each passage. Study each one in context one by one. What does this phrase really mean? What is God saying to you about it? Write down your insights. As you learn the context of each passage, a clear understanding of that topic will begin to form.

W—Waiting and Repeating: A third way to approach Scripture is to find a verse that stands out to you, write it down, and then "walk around it" for a while. Read it, reread it, memorize it, pray it, and worship God with the truth contained in it. This method will help engrave that truth deeply on your heart.

Create a list of key verses that have spoken to you and include it in a folder you can bring with you for your time with God. Over the course of a few months, you will have collected a list of scriptures that God has highlighted. Take time to walk around them. Remind yourself of the truth they contain.

I've found it helpful to create a schedule for how I approach Scripture during my time with God. This helps me stay intentional and keeps my daily pursuit of God fresh. For example, on Monday, Wednesday, and Friday, I'll focus my time in the Scriptures on systematic reading. On Tuesday and Thursday, I'll spend that time on a one-topic study, and on Saturday and Sunday, I'll take time to wait and repeat. Each day, I will seek to spend around half of my time with God interacting with the Scripture. The other half I will spend in prayer.

Prayer

I've found that three types of prayer keep me focused. Just as we *SOW* God's truth into our hearts, we also *DIG* deeper with him through prayer.

D—Demonstrate Your Love: Demonstrating your love for God is called *worship*. This is time to recalibrate your heart toward him, taking yourself out of the center of your thoughts and putting God there. Don't wait until you feel it. Use your words and your body posture to worship God, and your spirit will stir. Sing a song. Lift your hands. Make a list of things you are thankful for and speak them out one by one.

Remember, God wants you to approach him as Father. Express a heart of thanks to God as honestly and authentically as you can. This can be a great time to use worship music. Sometimes it's effective to just be still. Take the time to lift up God above all else.

I—Intercession and Requests: One of the greatest mysteries in Scripture is that God has chosen to move on the earth in response to believing prayer. Prayer has the power to change the outcome of events and change the landscape of our hearts.

One type of prayer is called *intercession*. To intercede means "to stand between." God invites his people to stand between the needs of life and the throne of heaven, asking him to move and work on the earth. Tragically, many Christians never take the time to request things from God, even though he has revealed his will and his heart on countless issues in life through the Scripture.

I often start with big requests and end with personal needs. I do this because I've found that, if I start with myself, I usually never get around to praying for the bigger things! So I'll begin by praying specific requests for things like nations, governments, cities, the persecuted, and the poor. Always try to use Scripture as a guide to pray the specific promises of God. After I've prayed for the world, I pray for the church—all across the nations and right where I live. I pray specifically for our local church, its leadership and its mission. Then I pray for family, friends, and neighbors. Lastly, I pray specific prayers for myself.

Here's the model I use:

THE WORLD, THE NATIONS, THE LOST, THE POOR

THE GLOBAL CHURCH, THE LOCAL CHURCH

MY FRIENDS, FAMILY, NEIGHBORS, COWORKERS

MY NEEDS & DESIRES

Some people skip praying for themselves altogether, thinking that it's arrogant to make personal requests. But Jesus said that nothing could be further from the truth! He wants you to pray for yourself, and you won't experience the fullness of his blessing until you learn to ask

(Matthew 7:7–11). Make specific, humble requests of God, and he will honor your prayers and respond. Write these requests down so you can cross them off when God resolves them.

G—Godly Confession: Godly confession has two distinct applications. First is the confession of sin. Take time to ask God to reveal any specific sins in your heart, then turn them over to God and forsake them. Is there someone you need to forgive? Is there someone you need to confront? This is a time to actively agree with what God says about sin. After you have confessed these sins to God, determine if you need to make any restitution with someone else, and follow through. Once you have confessed your sins, make the choice to fully trust in God's forgiveness.

The second application of godly confession is confessing out loud *your identity in Christ*. Search the Scripture for what it says about who you are in him. Begin to memorize these verses, and allow God's truth to inform your sense of identity. Scripture tells us that we are *complete in him* (Colossians 2:10), we are *free from sin's power* (Romans 6:14), we have *access to God* (Ephesians 3:12), we are *not condemned* (Romans 8:1–2), and we are *forgiven* (Colossians 2:13).

Just speaking these confessions will have a profound impact on your emotional and mental states. I've often come into my time with God tired and timid and left refreshed and focused simply by confessing over my life what he has said. Confessions speak to the invisible world around you and change the atmosphere of the soul. Make a list of scriptures that declare who God says you are, and then regularly speak them out loud.

Just as you did with reading Scripture, you can create a schedule that rotates through these ways of praying. If you find your mind wandering and you're having a hard time staying focused, keep things moving by spending less time on each part. With the tools we have just outlined, you can begin building or strengthening your plan for a daily habit of seeking God.

There will be days when it feels like God is ten thousand miles away, but it's those days when God is especially reshaping and maturing your heart. The goal of this habit is not to create a perfect routine. Rather, it is to create opportunity for deep relationship.

Habit 1 serves as a foundation for the next six habits. But in order for your time with God to come alive, it will require one more critical element.

The Spark That Starts a Fire

We all know that a great fire can begin with just a tiny spark. Fire grows when it's given fuel, but what is the spark that can set your time with God ablaze? In one word, your time with God will require *expectation*. God will always meet you at your level of expectation. You must approach him every morning, believing that he will meet you there.

Jesus taught that whatever we ask in prayer we will receive if we have faith (Matthew 21:22), and God promises to be found by those who seek him with all their hearts (Jeremiah 29:13). Let it be done according to *your* faith. These statements can feel too far-reaching, or even dangerous, but every Christian must wrestle with the fact that *Jesus* spoke them. What if God is just waiting for someone to take him at his word? If you will bring an attitude of expectation into your daily meeting with God, he will meet you there and your life will never be the same.

Right now, God extends the invitation to you: Will you rearrange your calendar to seek him for an hour every morning? What do you really have to lose? Consider all you have to gain.

Father, I choose to seek you with all my heart. I am willing to rearrange my routine so that I can make relationship with you the first priority in my life. Help me, meet me, change me, in Jesus's name.

Chapter Four

THE HABIT OF RADIANCE

Sharing your faith as a way of life

"Walk in wisdom toward outsiders, making the best use of the time. Let your speech always be gracious, seasoned with salt, so that you may know how you ought to answer each person."

Colossians 4:5–6

I like to be comfortable. I like comfortable clothes; I like comfortable furniture; I like comfortable conversations. I really like comfort foods.

Comfort has been pushing its way up the priority list in the lives of most people in the Western Hemisphere for the last three hundred years. Did you know that toilet paper was invented in 1857? That might feel like a long time ago to you, but in the scope of history, it's not so far in the past. There was a lot of living and dying before 1857, and toilet paper was not a part of the equation. The modern toothbrush didn't become popular until 1938. Could you go a week without your toothbrush and toilet paper? For the sake of those closest to you, I hope not.

I've found in my own life that, shortly after a new comfort is introduced, it quickly moves in my mind from privilege to necessity. I remember the day the movie theater near my house swapped out its typical movie theater seats for brand-new leather La-Z-Boy recliners. The first time we experienced the new seats, we thought we were in a palace! A few weeks later though, when my family went to a different theater and was forced to sit in the normal spongy, sticky chairs, everyone in our family couldn't stop complaining!

Comfort has become such a priority in our culture that it deeply influences what we are willing to think or talk about. Uncomfortable conversations are often pushed down the priority list. Uncomfortable thoughts are often left for some future date.

When I was a little kid, I learned the prayer "Now I lay me down to sleep." It ended with the phrase "If I should die before I wake, I pray the Lord my soul to take." But that's a pretty uncomfortable idea. Who wants to think about dying? Who wants to consider the eternal resting place of the soul? So someone decided to change the last line so that it now reads "Guide me, Jesus, through the night and wake me with the morning light." Now you're talking. Give me that La-Z-Boy chair.

This obsessive affection for comfort has deeply influenced our spirituality, and the culture of our day has created some clear guidelines for religion. In most social circles, no one will fault you for holding to a deep personal faith. But it's important that you keep it *personal*. Don't *proselytize*. Don't push your beliefs on someone else.

I remember, as a brand-new Christian, being so excited about my faith. Jesus was changing my life and I wanted the world to know. I sat down with a few of my friends and started sharing everything I had learned. Soon the room grew awkwardly quiet. One of my friends said, "Wait, I respect your spiritual beliefs, but you're not trying to convert me, are you?" Well, yeah, I was, but I hadn't really thought it through. They all looked at me with mildly offended glares. Now things were uncomfortable.

Our society as a whole has embraced what sociologists call *expressive individualism*. This is the conviction that one belief or religion cannot be better or more true than any other. To think that your belief is better than someone else's is the very essence of arrogance and intolerance. In previous generations, to be tolerant meant to treat others with respect even when you believed that their convictions were wrong. But today, to be tolerant means to accept all beliefs as equally true and valid.

This leaves the follower of Jesus in an incredibly difficult position. We believe that God became a man and gave his life for the sins of the world. We believe that he rose again and that each individual must personally turn to him in order to receive forgiveness of sins and eternal life. Jesus boldly decreed that he is the way, the truth, and the life. You can't spin that.

In one sense, the gospel is amazingly inclusive: all people every-where, from every race, color, and background, are invited to receive God's grace. But in another sense, his call is incredibly exclusive. You must come to him. There's no other path to salvation. And you must come by way of the cross. This leaves followers of Jesus looking uncom-fortably out of step with the times.

Do the assumptions of our culture actually make sense? Upon investigation, the contradiction within the popular view of tolerance surfaces. If someone claims that all beliefs are equally valid and true, isn't *that* a belief in and of itself? And if you consider anyone who doesn't hold to *your* belief to be wrong, isn't that showing a lack of tolerance? Isn't that person's belief as valid and true as anyone else's? So how can it be wrong? Aren't the proponents of tolerance doing exactly what they demand that others don't? In other words, to require this kind of tolerance is to actually be incredibly intolerant.

D. A. Carson noted:

> The only thing that you are allowed to hate is intolerance as they define it, which shows that the whole system is, in some way or other, logically self-defeating ... It becomes intellectually bankrupting, because it becomes impossible to talk about ideas. They are automatically black-listed under the rubric intolerant.[21]

What is a follower of Jesus supposed to do in an environment like this? I think, if we're honest, most Christians don't spend a whole lot of time wrestling with that question. We've got bills to pay and problems to worry about. We also have the pressing social expectation to maximize our own comforts. It's far easier to go about your daily life and hardly ever talk about Jesus with those who are far from him.

But under all of our busyness, the Spirit of God within every believer calls us to share with others the truth of his grace. Dr. Timothy Keller observed that "anybody who's actually encountered *the real Biblical God* ... is always propelled out.... If you do not sense that you're propelled out ... almost under an inner compulsion ... to bear witness to the life-changing, world-changing relationship with God, [then] you haven't gotten one."[22]

As you grow in habit 1, developing a closer relationship with Jesus, something inside you will propel you out. That something is the *love* of God. You will find yourself interacting with others who are far from

God, and the Spirit of Jesus within you will tug on your soul. How can you stand by and say nothing? How can you watch your friend or your neighbor struggle without a living relationship with God and never broach the topic? As the love of God grows within you, it will push you beyond what is comfortable.

The apostle Paul outlined in his letter to the Romans the most important discomfort of the Christian life: "I speak the truth in Christ—I am not lying, my conscience confirms it through the Holy Spirit—I have great sorrow and unceasing anguish in my heart. For I could wish that I myself were cursed and cut off from Christ for the sake of my people" (Romans 9:1–3 NIV).

Paul used the phrase "unceasing anguish" to refer to an emotion that is so compelling that it overrides all his propensities to avoid uncomfortable situations. His heart ached for their salvation. Throughout his letters, Paul frequently taught that Christians should be happy. We should rejoice in the Lord always. But along with joy, we must also allow our hearts to experience this inner anguish. Although this sounds contradictory, our hearts can actually do both simultaneously. How else could we rejoice in God *always* and experience *unceasing* anguish?

As we learn to love God more deeply, that love will always drive us to face reality. And there is one reality that sets the human heart on fire and pushes us beyond our comforts: the reality of *hell*. Paul was expressing the emotionally devastating truth that some of the people he loved were on their way to hell.

Looking Hell in the Face

Hell is probably the most unmanageable, difficult topic in all of Scripture. We believe in heaven—there's little debate about that. But the reality of hell is so offensive and heinous that it almost instantly crashes our central nervous system. We just can't get our heads around it.

. . . .

We believe in heaven—there's little debate about that. But the reality of hell is so offensive and heinous that it almost instantly crashes our central nervous system.

. . . .

I've found that most followers of Jesus fall into one of three categories when it comes to hell. First, there are those who don't believe that hell exists. They believe in Jesus, heaven, and forgiveness, but they stop at hell. They ask, "How could a loving God condemn someone for eternity?" And their conclusion is that he can't. This is appealing for a number of reasons, and it solves a lot of problems. There's no need for unceasing anguish if no one is going to go to hell.

The trouble with this view is that it requires us to edit out massive sections of Scripture. Paul wrote about the return of Christ, saying, "This will happen when the Lord Jesus is revealed from heaven in blazing fire with his powerful angels. He will punish those who do not know God and do not obey the gospel of our Lord Jesus. They will be punished with everlasting destruction and shut out from the presence of the Lord and from the glory of his might" (2 Thessalonians 1:7–9 NIV).

I've read a number of theological explanations of this passage, but the message seems painfully clear: hell is real. There really is a place of eternal darkness and separation from God for those who do not come to Christ. Jesus took the topic of hell so seriously that he told us we would be better off plucking out our eyes or sawing off our hands than walking down the path to hell (Matthew 5:29–30). To edit hell out of the Bible requires a significant amount of theological cutting and pasting.

The second category are those who say they believe in hell but live as if it doesn't exist. We often fall into this category without realizing it. When cornered, many Christians would affirm that they believe the words of the Bible about hell. But we haven't spiritually experienced the reality of *unceasing anguish* for people who are headed toward it. Hell is not disrupting our daily lives or forcing us out of our comfort zones. This is probably the most common category of Christ followers today.

Tragically, avoiding the reality of hell stops our hearts from experiencing a deeper spiritual love. Although a belief in a literal hell will drive you to your knees and cause immense discomfort, it will also widen your heart and intensify your love for others.

So we are left with the third category: those who walk into the storm. We allow the truth about hell to shake us and change us. We revisit it often and learn to ache for those who are far from God—and pray like heaven depends on our words.

Scripture teaches that hell is a real place (Revelation 21:8) and that those who reject Christ will experience eternal torment and separation from God (Matthew 25:46). We are told that God does not want to send anyone to hell (1 Timothy 2:4), that hell was originally for Satan and his demons (Matthew 25:41), and that God's justice requires judgment for sin (Romans 3:26). This all makes the sacrifice of Jesus that much more lovely. Christ experienced the wrath of God on our behalf so that God's justice could be satisfied and his love could be displayed through the invitation of grace.

Paul talked about his burden for those who were far from God, then he used the rest of Romans 9 to teach on God's sovereignty. He wanted us to face the fact that we can't save anyone ourselves—God must do it. Yet the sovereignty of God is not an excuse for our passivity, because God wants us to carry a burden for the lost with him.

That's why Paul said in Romans, "Brothers, my heart's desire and prayer to God for them is that they may be saved" (Romans 10:1). He knew that God was ultimately in control, but he also knew that God has chosen to run the world in partnership with believing prayer and acts of faith. Your words and actions make a difference in the eternity of the people around you!

This is why every honest follower of Jesus must learn to step beyond what is comfortable and share the love of Christ. We must ask God to soften our hearts and deepen our love for others—but this request is dangerous. Real love is risky. You can get hurt. You might be rejected. C. S. Lewis wrote:

> To love at all is to be vulnerable. Love anything and your heart will be wrung and possibly be broken. If you want to make sure of keeping it intact, you must give it to no one, not even to an animal. Wrap it carefully round with hobbies and little luxuries; avoid all entanglements; lock it up safe in the casket or coffin of your selfishness. But in that casket—safe, dark, motionless, airless—it will change. It will not be broken; it will become unbreakable, impenetrable, irredeemable.[23]

Are you willing to risk vulnerability and begin to love others as Christ loves them?

Psychologists have discovered a phenomenon in human biology. When two lovers sit down next to each other, the beating of their hearts will synchronize. It does not occur when two strangers sit down in the same place.

The closer you get to God, the more your heart will align with his. You will begin to feel what he feels. His deep, burning affection for the lost will start to mess up your life. You will weep in prayer. You will be unwilling to sit back and do nothing. Soon, your love for others will propel you past your comforts and self-preservation. And your life will never be the same.

Learning to Share

How does a follower of Jesus talk to people about Christ in a culture like ours? For many of us, this is where things get difficult. We've all seen well-meaning Christians talk about Jesus in a way that made us want to distance ourselves as quickly as possible.

I've found that ineffective witnessing usually takes one of three forms: there's the Sergeant, the Salesman, and the Sage. The Sergeant is the person who smashes Jesus down everyone's throat, like a brash military officer. You may find this witness on the side of the road with a sign that reads "Repent or burn." In our culture, nothing is more unpalatable than this approach.

You will often hear someone who embraces the Sergeant mentality say things like "Well, Jesus offended people, so I'm just living like Jesus." Jesus offended *religious* people. Although he never compromised, sinners were drawn to Jesus. He didn't sugarcoat anything, but when they were with him, sinners felt *loved*.

Almost as unappealing as the Sergeant is the Salesman. This is the person who talks about Christ as if he were a no-money-down loan from the credit union. He's got brochures and a slick promotional spiel. Though his intentions may be good, our culture is allergic to salesmanship.

Haven't you experienced this in your own life? You're walking down a busy street and someone approaches you and says, "Excuse me, can I interest you in a free vacation?" How do you respond to someone like that? If you're like me, you don't even wait to hear what the person has to say. You've already decided that the offer is too good to be true and there must a catch. Salesmanship just doesn't work.

The third ineffective strategy for sharing about Jesus is the Sage. This is the person who talks to non-Christians about spirituality and wholeness but never gets around to talking about Jesus. The Sage may give his or her friends advice about their dating lives or talk about the practice of meditation, but the cross and the resurrection never make it into the conversation.

The Sage approach is not all bad. Some of the conversations could lead to real impact, but far too often, the Sage won't take the conversation to Christ. That topic feels too divisive and uncomfortable. And so the impact is muted.

In order to make a real difference for Jesus in this world, we need to push past the strategies of Sergeant, Salesman, and Sage. We need to inform our thinking on this topic with truth that transcends our present cultural environment.

Paul's advice is incredibly helpful:

> Continue steadfastly in prayer, being watchful in it with thanksgiving. At the same time, pray also for us, that God may open to us a door for the word, to declare the mystery of Christ ... that I may make it clear, which is how I ought to speak.

> Walk in wisdom toward outsiders, making the best use of the time. Let your speech always be gracious, seasoned with salt, so that you may know how you ought to answer each person. (Colossians 4:2–6)

What should we do before we share about Jesus? According to Paul, we should pray. We looked at some of the forms of prayer in the last chapter. When you make time for intercession and requests, it's important to pray specifically for those who are far from God. Pray that they will be saved (Romans 10:1). Pray that God opens their eyes (2 Corinthians 4:4). Pray for the right words to say and for an open door.

· ·

What should we do before we share about Jesus? According to to Paul, we should pray.

· ·

If you want to understand God's heart for the lost, then you need to be specific and intentional in this area of prayer. I keep a list of at least five names of people in my life who are far from God and pray for them by name throughout the week. Can you think of five people right now?

If you will pray for them regularly, at least two things will happen. First, God will begin to change your heart. You will think of their spiritual states more often and become more aware of their need for God. You will become less self-absorbed and more others-centered. Your heart will begin to align with God's heart of love. Second, God will change their hearts. He will draw them in through inexplicable ways and will work through your prayers of faith. You can't save them—only God can. But making a difference for Christ in the lives of others begins with simple, consistent prayer.

Next, Paul instructs us on what to say, and his advice is not exactly what we might expect. He doesn't give us a script to recite or points to memorize. He doesn't challenge us to carry around tracts or hand out Bibles. Instead, we are told to "walk in wisdom toward outsiders, making the best use of the time."

What is wisdom? Wisdom isn't a collection of helpful sayings and slogans or a pile of knowledge that is transferred through a monologue. Wisdom is using the *right* knowledge at the *right* moment. In other words, we must learn to custom-fit the unchanging truths of Jesus to the ever-changing environment around us. Wisdom requires that you listen, that you're attentive, and that you're winsome in your approach.

When Jesus met the Samaritan woman at the well, he didn't begin the conversation with "Hello, I know you've had five husbands and you're now living in sexual sin." He knew those facts about the woman, but it was using wisdom to withhold that information at the beginning. Instead, he began the conversation with a request. "Give me a drink" (John 4:7). Simple, practical, reasonable.

Jesus then grabbed her attention by saying, "If you knew the gift of God, and who it is that is saying to you, 'Give me a drink,' you would have asked him, and he would have given you living water" (John 4:10). Do you see what he was doing? He was connecting her *felt* need (thirst) to her *spiritual* need (grace) and doing it in a way that piqued her interest. Pretty soon, she opened her heart, humbled herself, confided in him, and believed that he was the Savior of the world! Amazing.

Paul is pushing us beyond evangelism scripts and Scripture quotes to lovingly engage people. Learn their story, listen to their heartbeat, and God will show you a key to unlock their interest. In fact, all you need to do is ask God for wisdom and he promises to give it to you (James 1:5). But then you have to actually *walk* in wisdom (Colossians 4:5). You have to leave your house every morning believing in faith that God will give you the wisdom you need to draw others to him.

If you will do that, he will begin to work powerfully. Before you know it, an opportunity to share about your relationship with God will pop up during a lunch with a coworker. Another opportunity will arise in the middle of a family get-together at your parents' house. It won't be long before the doors start swinging open.

Once we start stepping out, Paul gives us some instruction on what we should talk about: "Let your speech always be gracious, seasoned with salt" (Colossians 4:6). Grace should be at the center of our conversations.

Think back for a moment on when the gospel first became real to you: what was it about Jesus that changed you? Did all your problems instantly disappear? Probably not. Were all your questions perfectly answered? Unlikely. I know in my life, the thing that changed me was a personal encounter with grace. I realized that I was far from God and I needed saving, and I received his forgiveness. When I trusted Christ, peace filled my heart!

Paul says that this is what you should talk about with those far from God. Don't try to answer all their questions or solve all their problems. Instead, let your speech be *gracious*—tell them about your encounter with grace! Share about what he has done for you and do it in a way that connects to their stories as you learn about them. Share humbly and winsomely, and watch how your encounter with grace leads to theirs.

Then Paul says to make sure your words are "seasoned with salt." Salt makes things taste better. Recently, I was sitting with my son eating french fries at a restaurant when he turned to me and asked, "Daddy, what are french fries made out of?" I told him that they were made of potatoes, and I could see the confusion on his face. He couldn't understand how a food he didn't like (potatoes) had been transformed into a food he loved (french fries). So he asked the obvious question: "What turns potatoes into french fries?" The answer? Salt! Salt amplifies flavor and makes bland potatoes into delicious french fries.

When you talk about Jesus, don't serve him like an uncooked potato. Talk about his goodness—how he heals the broken, delivers the oppressed, and befriends the lonely. Tell people how good he is!

One of the biggest mistakes many followers of Jesus make is to progressively isolate ourselves from people far from God. In an attempt to grow in holiness, we often lose touch with those who aren't pursuing Jesus. Although it's important to guard against old temptations, avoiding those in your life who are far from God will sabotage God's purpose. He has placed you in relationship with those people so you can make a difference.

We are encouraged to live "without blemish *in the midst* of a crooked and twisted generation, among whom you shine as lights in the world" (Philippians 2:15). How can we make a difference in the lives of people if we're never *in the midst*?

The opportunities are everywhere once you begin to look—at work, at school, in your neighborhood, at the gym, and at your kid's soccer game. God has woven opportunities into the seemingly average moments of everyday life. But if you insulate your life from anyone who is broken and in need of grace, it's unlikely you will find many opportunities to make a real difference.

Finding the Kairos

In the middle of his instructions about sharing our faith, Paul tells us that we should be "making the best use of the time" (Colossians 4:5). The Greek language has two words to express the concept of time. The first is the word *chronos*, which refers to chronological time that is measured in hours, minutes, or seconds. If someone asked, "What time does the train arrive?" they would use the word *chronos*.

But the New Testament often uses the other Greek word to express the concept of time. It's the Greek word *kairos*, which literally means a supreme moment, an appointed time, or a moment in which God intervenes. When Paul instructs us to make the best use of the time, he doesn't use the word *chronos*; he uses *kairos*. He is saying, "Make the best use of supreme moments." Not all time is created equal. God has woven into each day supreme moments—moments where someone's heart is open or someone's soul is ready—and you have been placed in that moment by God to share your story of grace.

For far too long, followers of Jesus have been hesitant around the idea of *evangelism*. Sometimes it's because we're too busy and we haven't let the reality of eternity sink in and change the way we think and feel. For some of us, evangelism immediately makes us think of the Sergeant, the Salesman, or the Sage. We don't want to be like that. Maybe you are deeply intimidated to share your faith because you just don't feel qualified. You don't feel like you know enough about God or the Bible to answer people's questions.

That's why Paul's instructions are so freeing. He gives us simple steps to get moving. First pray, then ask for wisdom, then share your experience with grace and tell others how good God has been to you. Don't wait until you're holy enough or feel qualified enough, because that day will never come.

If you will step out and begin sharing *now*, something supernatural will happen in your life. Whether you have been following Jesus for thirty years or thirty days, sharing your faith will ignite a spiritual fire on the inside. In fact, I have never met a Christian who was spiritually tepid who regularly shared their faith. They don't exist! Sharing about Christ changes the world within you as it changes the world around you.

The more openly you share, the more deeply you will love and the more real your own faith will become. Your fears will start to melt away, and a new confidence in Jesus will grow. Sharing your faith will humble you, drive you to your knees, and grow a dependence and assurance in your heart like nothing else. Above all, sharing your faith will deepen and widen your love.

Habit 1 challenged us to spend the first hour of the morning alone with God. But don't stop there. It serves as a foundation to build a life with Jesus so that you can actually make a difference in the world. Habit 2 gives application to your growing love for God and stretches your faith in extraordinary ways.

Habit 2: *Share your faith every week.*

You might read this and think, *Share my faith once a week? Are you serious? I don't share my faith once a year!* Maybe this seems unrealistic right now, but let me assure you, *you can do this.* Start moving out in this direction and God will meet you. He will open up unexpected doors and stand with you even when your voice is shaky and you feel unqualified.

The first time I ever shared my faith, I gave the worst explanation of the gospel in the history of the world. But when I had finished, my friend Franky looked at me and said, "Yeah, I want to accept Jesus." I was shocked! God had used my clumsy, uninformed presentation of grace to move my friend to faith in Christ!

I prayed with him a simple prayer:

"Jesus, today I surrender. I believe you died and rose again. I receive forgiveness and eternal life. Be the king of my life from this day forward. Amen."

I've had the honor of praying that prayer with other people over the years. They aren't magic words. They're just an expression of a heart turning to Christ.

God will use you in ways you never imagined if you will extend a simple invitation.

Extending the Invitation

How much of your life has been shaped by the power of an invitation? I met my wife because someone invited me to a party. I started playing music because a friend invited me to join his band. I gave my life to Jesus because a preacher invited me to the front of the room for prayer. I got involved in ministry because my pastor invited me on a mission trip. Nearly every aspect of my life has been deeply impacted by the power of an invitation.

In 1955, a twenty-six-year-old preacher was invited to a small gathering of concerned citizens. When the preacher arrived, the organizer of the meeting asked him if he would be willing to oversee a citywide bus boycott. Martin Luther King Jr. said yes, and the rest is history.[24]

There are few things on Earth as powerful as a simple invitation. In John chapter 1, Jesus interacted with four people and gave each one an invitation to follow him. His interaction serves as a model for us today as we invite people to receive God's grace.

Invite the seeker to explore. The story begins with two men who followed Jesus because they heard John the Baptist speaking highly of him. They wanted to scope Jesus out, but they were too timid to ask him their questions directly. So instead they asked, "Teacher, where are you staying?" Jesus replied, "Come and you will see" (John 1:38–39). He took them back to where he was staying, and they shared a meal together.

He didn't force himself on them, but instead he let them meander around his house and just be with him. These men were seekers—open to God but not yet convinced that they could trust him—so Jesus invited the seekers to explore. He intentionally created a safe environment for spiritual exploration.

This is critical for those who want to know more but aren't yet sure what they believe. The key is to create time and space to just be together. Work on a project together or grab lunch together. During this time, allow the seeker to see you as you truly are: imperfect, flawed, but honest in your pursuit of God. Authenticity and vulnerability will create the opportunity for deeper conversation.

Invite ordinary people into an extraordinary life. Next, Jesus was introduced to Simon, and the first thing Jesus did was change his name. He said, "You are Simon the son of John. You shall be called Cephas" (John 1:42).

What was Jesus up to? The name Simon was a very common Hebrew name at the time, but Cephas, or Peter, was unique. It meant "the rock." He was calling out of Peter a new identity, inviting him to leave behind the safe, ordinary life of catching fish. He could be average, everyday Simon—or he could be *The Rock*. Which would you choose?

Everyone around you is searching for a bigger purpose, and following God is exciting, so hint at that excitement throughout your conversation and allow the adventure of God to draw others in.

Invite the outsider into community. Then, Jesus met Philip. Interestingly, Philip was from the same village where Andrew and Peter came from. Andrew went and found Peter, but it seemed no one thought to go tell Philip. Instead, Jesus himself decided to go to Galilee and track Philip down (John 1:43). Philip was the only one mentioned who was directly pursued by Jesus and seemingly forgotten by everyone else. Maybe Philip was an outsider. Maybe he was the type of guy who didn't have a long list of close friends. Do you know anyone like that?

All around you, at your job and in your neighborhood, there are people who are longing for real community. They want to be known. They want to build friendship. But they're waiting for a simple invitation. If you would invite them to go with you to church or come over for dinner, they would jump at the opportunity.

Invite the skeptic into a personal encounter. Lastly, Jesus met Nathanael. When Nathanael heard about Jesus, he was skeptical. His first reaction was to ask, "Can anything good come out of Nazareth?" (John 1:46). Nathanael knew Nazareth was a poor town that was hardly mentioned in the prophetic Scriptures, so when he met Jesus, his guard was up.

"Jesus saw Nathanael coming toward him and said of him, 'Behold, an Israelite indeed, in whom there is no deceit!' Nathanael said to him, 'How do you know me?' Jesus answered him, 'Before Philip called you, when you were under the fig tree, I saw you.' Nathanael answered him, 'Rabbi, you are the Son of God!'" (John 1:47–49).

This is interesting. When dealing with a skeptic, Jesus didn't seem to directly answer any of Nathanael's concerns. He didn't explain how he was originally from Bethlehem, the prophesied birthplace of the coming Savior. He didn't tell Nathanael about the virgin birth, the wise men, or the star that rested over the manger. Instead, he told Nathanael that he had seen him under a fig tree.

What does that mean? What was Nathanael doing under that tree that was relevant in this moment, and why would Jesus bring that up? The truth is, we don't know. We have no idea why that fact was relevant. Only Jesus and Nathanael knew, and it was so personal and so relevant that mentioning it to Nathanael transformed a staunch skeptic into a passionate believer in an instant.

Do you know any skeptics in your life? God can soften their hearts with one personal encounter. Do you know any outsiders or seekers? Do you know anyone who is bored with the mundane routines of an ordinary life? I'm sure you do. What could happen in their lives if you just extended an invitation?

Begin with daily prayer, asking God for open doors of opportunity and divine wisdom. Live in the midst, cultivating honest relationship with those in your circle of influence who are far from God. Learn their stories, and build honest, humble relationships. Look for *kairos* moments, where the conversation can turn to deeper things, and step out and share about your encounter with grace. Then humbly, courageously, extend an invitation.

Do this once, and your heart will begin to come alive. Do it twice, and your day will be injected with a new level of energy. Do it every week, and living for God will take on a great sense of adventure and your spiritual growth will shoot through the roof. I've found in my own life that nothing grows the heart like sharing your faith. Nothing.

Years ago, the great preacher D. L. Moody preached a compelling sermon and ended with a challenge. "Come back tomorrow," Moody said, "and I will tell you how you can receive salvation and forgiveness." That was October 8, 1871, the night of the Great Chicago Fire. Dozens of people who heard Moody's sermon that night went back to their homes and died in the flames.

Moody would later write of the experience, "I want to tell you one lesson I learned that night which I have never forgotten, and that is when I preach to press Christ upon the people then and there, I try to bring them to a decision on the spot. I would rather have that right hand cut off than give an audience a week to decide what to do with Jesus."[25]

The reality of eternity demands that we live with a sense of urgency. People around you are far from God. What will you do about it?

Jesus, I want to share my faith every week. Wake me up; open the doors of opportunity; change my heart. I say yes. Use me, God, as you never have before.

Chapter Five

THE HABIT OF RECEPTIVITY

Learning the voice of the Holy Spirit

"The Lord said to him in a vision, 'Ananias.'
And he said, 'Here I am, Lord.'"

Acts 9:10

We believe in a God who can do the impossible. He is the God of miracles. He is the God who speaks through a burning bush, parts the Red Sea, drops manna from heaven, and causes the walls of Jericho to fall down. He raises the dead and walks on water. He intervenes in the affairs of everyday life.

Most followers of Jesus would agree with this conviction. We believe that God *can* do anything. But there seems to be a gap between what we say we believe and what we actually experience. For many of us, the God of supernatural intervention feels more like a theory and less like a living, breathing reality. That kind of life is *possible*; it just seems to be reserved for certain special people.

A while ago, Netflix released a series called *The Crown*. The show chronicles the life of the royal family of England through the highs and lows of the last seventy-five years. The series gives the Hollywood version of the Queen, her siblings, and all the tensions that come with living every moment in the spotlight.

The deeper you get into the story, the more one truth becomes blatantly obvious: there is nothing normal about the life of the royal family. The places they go, the things they do, the problems they face. The people in Buckingham Palace live in a bubble unlike any other on Earth. They are the epitome of the *elite*. They have access, opportunity, power, and resources—more than most of us could ever imagine.

Our world constantly draws a line between the "haves" and the "have-nots." In high school, there were the cool kids and the less-than-cool kids. The cool kids got invited to the party, played leading roles on the sports teams, and were always surrounded by a crowd of friends. The less-than-cool kids got skipped over. In some families, there is the "good sibling" and the "other siblings." One of the kids in the house usually gets disproportionately more attention, praise, and opportunity. Professional sports teams have the stars who receive multimillion-dollar contracts, and they have the guys on the bench who are making a fraction of the money.

In nearly every area of life, you can find the divide between those who are considered to be *in* and those who are considered to be *out*.

And throughout history, the church, along with the rest of society, has tragically followed this rule. In fact, the church has given names to the *in* group and the *out* group. The clergy are often seen as those who have special access to God, while the laity are the common, ordinary people. This distinction leads many Christians to internalize a lethal assumption: that God speaks to and works in the lives of the special spiritual people—but you aren't one of them. You shouldn't expect to personally hear from God or see biblical-sized miracles in your life.

Along with the clergy-laity divide, some teachers of the Bible would say that God has once and for all spoken through his Word and now has nothing more to say to us about our present lives. We shouldn't expect to hear from God or interact with him personally. This view comes with some significant problems, one of which is that while supporting the validity and supremacy *of* Scripture, the proponent of this perspective undermines the actual example set *by* Scripture.

Theologian Dallas Willard rightly noted:

> The close of the scriptural canon marks the point in the (still ongoing) divine-human conversation where the principles and doctrines that form the substance of Christian faith and practice are so adequately stated in human language that nothing more need to be said in general. Biblical Christians believe that nothing further will be said by God to extend or contradict these principles. But biblical Christians are not just people who hold certain beliefs about the Bible. They are also people who lead the kind of life demonstrated in the Bible: a life of personal, intelligent interaction with God.[26]

You can't fully obey the life model taught in the Bible without believing in a God who speaks, works, and moves today. To close your mind and heart off to God's personal direction is to functionally adhere to a form of biblical deism—believing in a present God who never actually makes himself presently known.

Tragically, those who live as though God never speaks also miss out on the sacred communion Christ came to secure. Brother Lawrence famously wrote, "There is not in the world a kind of life more sweet and delightful than that of a continual conversation with God."[27] What if the Scripture was not intended to simply be an almanac of days gone by, but rather a catalog of possibilities? What if God wants to guide us throughout the day, and what if following his guidance dramatically increases the number of miracles we experience?

Consider the overarching example of Scripture. God spoke to Adam, Cain, Noah, Abraham, Sarah, Moses, Gideon, and David. He spoke to Mary, Peter, Paul, Stephen—and on and on! Hundreds of accounts of God breaking into the human story and engaging in real-life conversations.

But the conversations didn't stop with the closing of the canon of Scripture. History is packed with accounts of men and women hearing from God and personally experiencing his power. You can read about the lives of Polycarp, Augustine, Martin Luther, John Wesley, Catherine Booth, Watchman Nee, Maria Etter, William Seymour, Billy Graham, and Mother Teresa. Each individual recorded times when God clearly spoke to them, and their testimonies make up only the smallest fraction of those who have held genuine conversations with God!

There's just one problem with all this evidence: the people I listed are all part of the *royal family*. They represent the spiritually elite. They have access to God that the rest of us common believers just don't have—at least that's what we've often believed.

Jesus taught that his followers would know his voice (John 10:27) and that his Spirit would guide us into all truth (John 16:13). Paul said that all of God's children would be led by the Spirit of God (Romans 8:14). The gospel tears down the wall between the haves and the have-nots. It's the story of the highest of the elite, namely

Jesus, becoming the lowest of the low and dying on the cross. He took the role of a commoner so that he could give us the gift of his Spirit, enabling us to experience the access of the elite. Hearing the voice of God is not reserved for Paul, Polycarp, Billy Graham, and Mother Teresa. It is the privilege of every son and daughter in the kingdom!

I love the story of Ananias in Acts chapter 9, when God knocked Saul of Tarsus off his feet and blinded his eyes. God spoke to Ananias to go and pray for Saul and lead him to faith in Christ. We are told, "Now there was a disciple at Damascus named Ananias. The Lord said to him in a vision, 'Ananias.' And he said, 'Here I am, Lord'" (Acts 9:10).

Notice how Ananias is described in the story. We aren't told that he was a great preacher or spiritual leader. He was not, to our knowledge, an overseer, pastor, or prophet. Instead, we are told that Ananias was a *disciple*. That means he was a Christian.

In other words, Ananias was a *guy*; an average, Jesus-loving guy! Maybe he worked at the Ford dealership down the street. Maybe he was the VP of marketing at the large corporation downtown. Maybe he was a college senior at the local university. The apostle Paul, who would go on to become the most fruitful, famous Christian in church history, was led to faith by a *guy* named Ananias!

Do you see the irony? Without Ananias, the churches Paul planted wouldn't have been planted. Paul wrote two-thirds of the New Testament—but none of that would have been written. History itself depended on a *guy* named Ananias obeying the prompting of the Holy Spirit and leading Saul of Tarsus to faith in Christ.

Ananias is an amazing example of the truth at the center of the gospel.

In the last days, God says,

   I will pour out my Spirit on *all* people.

Your sons *and* daughters will prophesy,

   your young men will see visions,

   your old men will dream dreams.

Even on my servants, both men and women,

   I will pour out my Spirit in those days,

   and they will prophesy.

I will show wonders in the heavens above

   and signs on the earth below. (Acts 2:17–19 NIV)

This is the promise for the people of God right now! God wants to pour his Spirit out on all flesh! He wants to give visions to men *and* women, rich *and* poor, old *and* young. His promise cuts down the gender lines, the racial lines, the economic lines, and the generational lines. God wants to speak to everyone and move through everyone, elite and non-elite alike.

But you won't experience the fullness of his power until you begin to believe that this power is actually for you!

Not So Easy

If you've ever stepped out in faith and asked God for his moment-by-moment guidance, you know that this can be a little messy. Maybe you've heard the stories or lived firsthand the reality of someone who *heard from God* but actually didn't hear from God.

As a pastor, I've encountered so many stories about people who claim to have heard from God but who really haven't—or who have misused their proclamation of it. Maybe Tom is sure he's heard from God that he's going to marry Angie—except God hasn't mentioned anything about it to Angie. Tom assures her that God has indeed made this pronouncement. And now ... they're married to other people.

This type of "hearing from God" can cause all kinds of hurt, manipulation, and confusion. It sometimes makes those who claim to be led by the Spirit lose credibility in the eyes of those around them. In addition, I've seen dozens of well-meaning Christians, desperate to hear and follow God's voice, adopt all kinds of unhelpful practices for attempting to hear it. There are those who follow the "Random Verse Method." Have you ever done this or known someone who has? It's when you need direction from God, so you flop open your Bible and expect the random page you now see to hold the key to your problem. The Random Verse Method is not a reliable strategy for hearing from God.

There's the "Fleece Method," also known as the "Open Doors Method." This is when a follower of Jesus will put out a "fleece" like Gideon did to determine God's will. For example, "If I get a hole in one today at mini-golf, I will see it as a sign from God that I should ask my girlfriend to marry me." Or, "If the company calls before 7:00 p.m. today, then I should take the job in Arizona." The Open Doors Method is a variant of the same: "If the door opens for us to buy the house, then it must be God's will to move forward. If the door closes, then we shouldn't buy the house."

Though well-intentioned, these methods for hearing God's voice can quickly create a world of confusion, uncertainty, and missteps. They rarely produce confident, faith-filled followers of Jesus, because they are fundamentally flawed in their premises. They work from the assumption that God is like a puppet master, seeking to control every movement of his puppets. Or that he's like a computer program. If you put in the right code, you will get the desired result.

But God is not a riddle that must be solved; he is a *Father who must be known*. Hearing from God flows from authentic relationship with him.

. . . .

Hearing from God flows from authentic relationship with him.

. . . .

When I first began my journey in following the Spirit, I would walk down the street and ask God to guide me any way he wanted. I told him that my desire was to obey his guidance 100 percent and nothing was off-limits. Soon, I'd feel an inner nudge that I thought might be from God. But then I'd feel another. Then another. I'd inwardly ask, "God, do you want me to go to the library across the street? Wait, are you asking me to talk about Christ with the man pumping gas over there? Or—did you just impress on me to pray for the elderly people at the assisted living facility down the road?"

It didn't take long before I was a tangled ball of confusion. I wanted so badly to do God's will, but all of those things seemed like good options. How can we know what God specifically wants us to do?

What I didn't understand at the time is that God never intended to create an army of robots. If God wanted us to live our lives mechanically following direction, then he wouldn't have given us the capacity for reason and choice. Instead, God made us in *his* image. He gave us creativity, intelligence, moral discernment, and initiative, because he doesn't want the programmed obedience of a robot—he wants the heart obedience of a son or daughter.

What parent would be pleased to find their eighteen-year-old son showing up at their bedroom door every morning to ask: "Mom, Dad, should I eat oatmeal or raisin bran for breakfast? Should I wear the green shirt or the blue one? Should I take the highway to work or the back roads?" These are decisions he can make on his own, and the success of the parent is seen in the ability of the son to decide maturely.

God made us free moral agents, and as a good father, he guides his children without controlling them. He wants us to learn to walk with him in a free, voluntary, humble way. And when we approach God from this perspective, his will for our lives is revealed more clearly.

The Three Wills

When theologians talk about the will of God, they are actually speaking of the "three wills" of God.

First, there is God's *sovereign will*. This refers to the perfect, secret plan of God that cannot be stopped. In the end, God will have his way. The Scripture teaches that "our God is in the heavens; he does all that he pleases" (Psalm 115:3) and "he does according to his will among the host of heaven and among the inhabitants of the earth; and none can stay his hand" (Daniel 4:35). Our response to the sovereign will of God must be a deep, inner surrender. He is God and we are not. We can trust his sovereign will because the God we trust is good.

Along with his sovereign will, there is also the *moral will* of God. We are told in the Scripture that it isn't his will that any should perish (2 Peter 3:9), yet some do. It isn't his will for people to commit murder or lie, yet some do. God's moral will is often broken by humanity, and ignoring his will comes with consequences.

God's moral will for your life is that you live holy, and your response to his moral will must be to learn his ways. Jesus said, "You will know the truth, and the truth will set you free" (John 8:32). It's the truth you know that sets you free. If you don't know it, it won't set you free. This is why we must learn God's moral will and, with his help, obey it.

Lastly, there is God's *unique will.* This is his personal plan for you. He cares about every detail in your life like a loving, liberating father does, and he wants to guide you. But until you are surrendered to his sovereign will and a student of his moral will, God's unique will is very difficult to discern. It makes no sense to ask him, "Lord, do you want me to leave my wife?" because he's already given you moral guidance on divorce in the Scripture. Before you can accurately receive his guidance, you must inwardly operate from a place of submission to what he has already revealed.

A. T. Pierson wrote about the power of meekness when it comes to hearing God's voice for personal direction:

> *Meekness is a real preference for God's will.* Where this holy habit of mind exists, the whole being becomes so open to impression that, without any *outward* sign or token, there is an *inward* recognition and choice of the will of God. God guides, not by a visible sign, but by *swaying the judgment.* To wait before Him, weighing candidly in the scales every consideration for or against a proposed course, and in readiness to see which way the preponderance lies, is a frame of mind and heart in which one is fitted to be guided; and God touches the scales and makes the balance sway as He will. *But our hands must be off the scales,* otherwise we need expect no interposition of His, in our favour.[28]

You must take your hands off the scales. As your heart develops an attitude of meekness, you are cultivating the inner environment that can discern the voice of God's Spirit. Deeper than emotion or intellect, this inner voice takes time to learn. "The spirit of man is the lamp of the LORD" (Proverbs 20:27). This means that God will speak to the inner person of your spirit as his Spirit communicates with you. Elijah described his voice as a still, small voice (1 Kings 19:12).

Four simple tests can help you avoid confusion when it comes to discerning God's voice.

> 1. *The Doctrine Test*. When trying to hear God's voice, first ask, "What does the Bible teach on this topic? Does my decision align with the teaching of Scripture?" Some questions can be completely answered through the Doctrine Test. For example, it's not God's will for you to lie to your boss about the report you didn't complete. You don't have to pray much about that one to know what God's will is. This is one area where the counsel of a pastor or other leader from your church can be helpful if you're uncertain about what the Bible teaches on a particular topic.
>
> 2. *The Disciple Test*. Next, ask, "Does this decision make me more like Jesus? Does it push me to trust God more? Will it stretch my heart to love him more?" Everything God leads you to do will in some way make you more like Christ. If the answer to this question is clearly *no*, then God's will is fairly obvious.
>
> 3. *The DNA Test*. Thirdly, ask, "Does this decision seem to fit with how God has been working in my life

recently?" You're looking for clues of the work of God's providential hand in your life. God can and will speak by unexpectedly aligning events or situations. Does this decision seem to be marked with a divine DNA? You need to learn to discern between coincidence and divine appointment. Sometimes, God will lead you to do something that is outside of your gift mix, so you can't write off an opportunity just because it's beyond your comfort zone. What is God doing in your life? The more you are aware of his overall guidance, the more clearly you can discern his specific guidance.

4. *The Dinner Table Test.* Lastly, ask, "When I sit down at the table with wise, mature Christians who know me and love me, what do they think of my decision?" Notice it doesn't ask, "When I sit down with friends who think just like me, what do they say?" Invite mature Christians into your process as you learn to discern God's voice. Their wisdom can save you a lot of needless pain. Here is again an area where your pastor or other leaders from your church can play a critical role. What do these leaders think about your decision?

These four tests will help you build a library of evidence when it comes to knowing and following God's voice. Over time, like in any relationship, you will become more and more familiar with the direction of God (John 10:27).

But familiarity isn't enough. To experience the fullness of life with God, familiarity must be combined with availability.

The Secret of Availability

When Ananias was instructed to go and pray for Saul of Tarsus, it's easy for us to imagine this moment as an extreme miracle. Did Jesus physically walk into Ananias's living room? Did heaven open and a voice come from the clouds? Maybe—but probably not. We read that he had a vision, but we aren't told anything about the specific way his vision manifested. It's possible that he just saw a picture in his mind's eye or even that the vision was more like a prompting or an impression.

My guess is that his vision was far more subtle and subjective than we might think. Maybe Ananias was just having his daily time of prayer and he felt a quiet tug in his spirit. He responded to God with the same four words that Abraham spoke when he was called. They're the same words that Moses said at the burning bush. In fact, they're the same words Jacob, Samuel, and Isaiah used when God spoke to them. These four words seem to serve as a passcode for anyone who wants to hear from God.

"Here I am, Lord."

Simple, right? At first glance, it's an easy phrase to pass over. But upon further investigation, we discover that these words are the beginning of a great adventure for Ananias, because they testify to the one characteristic that matters most to God: *availability*. God always chooses available people. John Wimber wrote, "The only thing required to be used of God to deliver a gift—be it healing, deliverance, prophecy—is to be available."[29]

Availability is the key ingredient God looks for, and it comes in various degrees. Think about your own life. You have different levels of availability for different people. Some people, when their numbers pop up on your phone, you quickly send the calls to voicemail. Others, you might take their calls only if you're working. We all have a few people who, when they call, we rush to answer, no matter when it is or where we are.

Would you answer God's call if he woke you up at three in the morning and asked you to pray? Could he call you while you're in an important business meeting? Could he call you on your day off?

In many ways, availability serves as an indicator of depth in a relationship. For those closest to us, our availability increases, so it serves as a good measuring stick to determine the true state of your relationship with God. Maybe you aren't seeing greater miracles or hearing God's voice simply because you haven't made yourself available. What will you do if he calls?

We don't know exactly what Ananias was doing when God spoke to him, but whatever he was doing, he was willing to stop. His response, "Here I am, Lord," tells us that he wanted to receive direction. I've found this to be so important in hearing the voice of the Holy Spirit. If you can't slow down to listen, you'll quickly find that God doesn't seem to speak to you very often.

The story of Samuel powerfully illustrates this point. In his first experience with the voice of God, Samuel mistook God's voice for the voice of his mentor, Eli (1 Samuel 3:4–5). It's easy to miss the voice of God because it often sounds like a familiar voice. It may sound like the thoughts in your head at first, and if you're unwilling to pause and listen, you will move right past it. Discerning God's voice requires that you slow down and linger.

Begin by praying, *"Here I am, Lord."* As you make yourself available and take the time to listen, the voice of God will stand out.

In the case of Ananias, God told him to go and pray for Saul of Tarsus, and the specificity of the command was amazing. He told Ananias which street to go to and which house Saul would be in (Acts 9:11). Sometimes,

God chooses to guide us with incredibly specific instruction, and we should be grateful for these moments.

Years ago, when our church had just started Sunday services and we were meeting in a local high school, I drove past an old, boarded-up theater in the downtown section of our city. As soon as my eyes read the sign "The Palace Theater," I felt the Spirit whisper to my heart, saying, "You're going to meet in that theater." Later that day, I went back with my two sons, and we laid our hands on the outside of the building and asked God to clarify his plan and swing open the door.

You will never guess what happened the next day.

Nothing happened.

In fact, nothing happened for over a year. But about eighteen months later, a pastor I didn't know, who also didn't know me, prayed for me at a local gathering of church leaders. He stopped in the middle of his prayer and asked me, "Are you a pastor?" I said, "Yes." Then he asked, "Do you lead a church that meets at a school but you've had your eyes on a theater?"

I hadn't told anyone. There's no way he could have known. Again, wide-eyed, I said, "Yes." He said, "God wants you to know that he's opening the door for you to meet in that theater." Miraculously, God did open the door, and twelve months later we held our first service in the theater. God had a plan, and he chose to be *incredibly specific*!

But God's leading isn't always that specific, and even when it is, it doesn't remove the feeling of risk. With all that specificity, Ananias was hesitant to obey.

> "Lord, I have heard from many about this man, how
> much evil he has done to your saints at Jerusalem.
> And here he has authority from the chief priests to

bind all who call on your name." But the Lord said to him, "Go, for he is a chosen instrument of mine to carry my name before the Gentiles and kings and the children of Israel. For I will show him how much he must suffer for the sake of my name." (Acts 9:13–16)

Ananias received a specific call from God, but he was still scared for his life. Saul of Tarsus was a known killer of Christians, and he had come to town with the intention of arresting every follower of Jesus.

Notice that when Ananias expressed his concern about his own safety, God responded by talking about Saul and not at all about Ananias. He didn't mention Ananias's safety even once! It was not that God didn't care. Rather, he was teaching Ananias that following his Spirit would not guarantee the absence of all danger. True safety in life is not the absence of danger—it's the *presence* of God. When you are following his guidance and seeking the center of his will, there is no safer place on Earth.

Imagine for a moment if Ananias hadn't gone. Paul had been blinded by the light he saw, and when Ananias arrived, he hadn't eaten or drunk anything for three days. What if Ananias had delayed, hesitating for a day or two, and then gone to see Saul of Tarsus? Most likely, Saul would have starved to death huddled in a corner! He might have died and become a footnote in history, all because one *guy* named Ananias wasn't willing to risk and obey God's voice.

It's a difficult truth to face, but *every miracle has an expiration date*. When we choose to live as though God isn't speaking, or when we ignore his voice because we are too busy, we are missing the moments that bring the power of heaven to the circumstances of Earth! These opportunities pass when God's people aren't led by his Spirit. Has God been leading you to talk to a family member about Jesus? Is he leading you to pray for a coworker who is sick? Is God leading you to invite your neighbor to church? These are the moments that launch us into a life of the miraculous.

Thank God that Ananias did not ignore the Holy Spirit. He gathered his courage, walked across town, and met Saul at the house where he was staying. When Ananias prayed for Saul, "immediately something like scales fell from his eyes, and he regained his sight. Then he rose and was baptized; and taking food, he was strengthened" (Acts 9:18–19).

This is the last time we read anything about Ananias in the Scripture, but his one step of faith set in motion the greatest move of God in history.

I love the language used to describe the miracle. It happened *immediately*. Much of Christian maturity is a slow process, taking years to develop, but not everything in our spiritual lives should happen slowly. God also uses *immediately*. These are the moments of instant breakthrough and change.

Wouldn't you like to see a few more *immediatelys* in your life? Wouldn't you like to see your loved one turn to Christ now? Or the healing you have been praying for happen? Or the financial breakthrough actually come to pass? Maybe you've noticed that some Christians seem to experience more *immediatelys* than others. Is it because God likes them more? Are they more holy, or part of the elite group? No. The story of Ananias teaches us that when normal people follow God's promptings, miracles will follow us.

If we would commit ourselves to learning the inner voice of the Spirit and living each day with a posture of availability, *immediately* moments would start interrupting our everyday lives.

Habit 1 teaches you to set the course of your day by starting it with God. Habit 2 teaches you to share your faith with those far from him. But habit 3 transforms your spiritual routines into a dynamic adventure and causes your life to resemble the New Testament model of a follower of Jesus.

Habit 3: *Obey the daily promptings of the Holy Spirit.*

Are you ready to obey the Holy Spirit's promptings throughout your day? Are you ready to give God permission to interrupt your plans? Are you ready to cultivate a deeper trust relationship with God?

Jesus frequently ended his sermons with the phrase "He who has ears to hear, let him hear" (Matthew 11:15 and 13:9, for example). He was emphasizing the important truth that we must intentionally give ourselves to spiritual listening.

Remember the story of Samuel, who mistook the voice of God for Eli's? Three times, Samuel heard God speak and thought it was Eli, but the fourth time he began a conversation with God. What changed that enabled Samuel to discern God's voice? After the third time God spoke, Eli instructed Samuel to go back to his room and listen for God. So Samuel went back, expecting God to speak. As we learned with habit 1, expectation opens the door for the supernatural. If you don't expect God to speak, you will often miss his promptings.

. . . .

If you don't expect God to speak, you will often miss his promptings.

. . . .

After Samuel returned to his room, God called his name again. But this time, rather than running to Eli, Samuel responded to God by saying, "Speak, for your servant hears" (1 Samuel 3:10).

Samuel specifically asked God to speak, and this is important. Jesus taught that whoever asks, receives, and that whoever seeks, finds (Matthew 7:7–11). There are blessings from God that you will never receive until you specifically ask. F. B. Meyer said, "The greatest tragedy of life is not unanswered prayer, but unoffered prayer." Are you asking God to speak to you throughout your day? If not, then it will be impossible to cultivate habit 3 in your life.

Samuel came to God with an expectation, asked God to speak, and then said, "Your *servant* hears." He called himself God's servant, demonstrating a deep reverence for God. This attitude of the heart cannot be overstated. Pride blocks the voice of God, and treating the things of God lightly will silence his voice in your life. When we revere God's Spirit, his voice is amplified, and Samuel's experience with God teaches us how to develop an *EAR* to hear.

- **E**xpect God to speak.
- **A**sk God to speak.
- **R**evere God in your heart.

Applying these three instructions daily will open up the possibility of a dynamic, Spirit-led life. God will begin to guide you. Miracles will begin to find you.

Following the promptings of his Spirit can make the difference between blessing and brokenness, favor and frustration—and even life and death.

Perhaps you've heard stories, as I have, of people who have come out of tragic situations and been transformed by Christ. But like a battlefield that has been made into a children's park after the war, some scars endure. Like the addict who cleans up her life and is about to regain custody of her children but has a relapse and dies of accidental overdose. Like the death-row criminal who is radically saved but who still has to endure the consequences of his old life.

Life is very short, and there are many things we will never understand. But in the midst of it all, God whispers to his children through the inner voice of his Spirit.

If you will *expect, ask,* and *revere,* his voice will become more and more clear in your heart. You are called to a dynamic life of spiritual adventure. You are called to a life of miracles.

Spirit of Jesus, I want to follow your promptings every day. Right now, I open my heart. Use my circumstances, my influence, and my relationships to bring the power of heaven to Earth. Speak, Lord; your servant hears. I give you full permission to interrupt my schedule. Here I am, Lord.

PART 3:
GUARD RAIL
HABITS

"Setting boundaries inevitably involves taking responsibility for your choices. You are the one who makes them. You are the one who must live with their consequences."[30]

Dr. Henry Cloud

"The public person I was wasn't a lie; it was just incomplete. When I stopped communicating about my problems, the darkness increased and finally dominated me. As a result, I did things that were contrary to everything I believe."[31]

Ted Haggard

"We, however, will not boast beyond proper limits."

Apostle Paul (2 Corinthians 10:13 NIV)

Chapter Six

THE HABIT OF RIGHTEOUSNESS

Living free from sexual brokenness

"The body is not meant for sexual immorality, but for the Lord, and the Lord for the body."

1 Corinthians 6:13

In the year 360 BC, the Greek philosopher Plato wrote about an ancient city that had existed nine thousand years before his time. He claimed that the city was unlike any other, with exquisite architecture, incomprehensible wealth, and unfathomable beauty. It was believed that this city was endowed with a certain magic from divine beings that made it a sort of utopia on Earth. But everything changed in an instant when the city suffered a great earthquake and flood that swept it into the sea.

It's been over two thousand years since Plato wrote his story of the ancient city, yet archaeologists and historians are still searching for the lost city of Atlantis.

What comes to mind when you hear the word *Atlantis*? For many of us, it conjures up feelings of mystery and intrigue. The idea of a beautiful lost city seems to speak to something deep in the recesses of our hearts. It's no wonder we have been searching for Atlantis for thousands of years: we want to believe in a place like this. We want to discover a place like this. And something inside us tells us that a place like this does actually exist—somewhere.

Just as historians and archaeologists obsess over Atlantis, our hearts seem to be in search of an invisible lost city. You may have never called it that before or even put words around what you feel, but there is something within all of us that seems to be searching.

But what are we searching for? We want to feel connected. We want to be deeply known.

Maybe you felt this inner search the first time you fell in love. It felt like you could fly, dance, and cry all at the same time. It felt like life finally made sense. Or maybe you felt it at the birth of your child. You held that tiny body in your arms and experienced a warmth like you had never known. Sometimes, we catch a glimpse of this feeling at the sight of a sunset or the ocean. In those moments, you feel like you belong.

And then the feeling fades. So you search again. What is it really that your soul is searching for? What is the lost city of the heart?

Deep down, you and I are searching for *intimacy*. Intimacy means to be close to someone else—so close that the boundaries between your individual selves blur. Falling in love, holding your newborn child, watching the sunrise—all of these moments carry the aroma of intimacy. But the connection is fleeting. Just when it becomes tangible, it seems to fade, and our hearts start hunting to find it again.

The first story in the Bible teaches us that the human race really did live in a spiritual Atlantis at one time. We were connected—close to God and one another. Man and God walked together in the garden in the cool of the day. Man and woman were naked and unashamed. Man himself was whole, without brokenness and fragmentation.

John Eldredge put it this way: "There was a time when Adam drank deeply from the source of all Love. He—our first father and archetype—lived in an unbroken communion with the most captivating, beautiful, and intoxicating Source of life in the universe. Adam had God."[32]

But you know the story. Sin entered the human equation, separating man from God, man from woman, and man from himself. Soon, humans couldn't meet their deep ache for intimacy and were forced to settle for less. Rather than seeking fulfillment through a genuine connection with God, the human race traded that pursuit for shadows and counterfeits. The idea of intimacy was flattened out, repackaged, and simplified.

Today, when the word *intimacy* is used, it is almost always associated with only one thing: sex.

Deep Implications

Think about the last time you heard the word *intimacy*. Was the person using it to mean anything close to the deep connection between God and your soul? Most likely, it had everything to do with sex. If a counselor asks a married couple, "How is your intimate life?" it's assumed he's talking about sex. If you search online for "intimate apparel," I don't think you will find hiking boots for those long, contemplative walks or a Bible study guide.

In our world today, intimacy simply means sex, and there's a deeper lesson that's being taught by the association of those two words. The cultural message is that, if you want to fill the void that's searching for intimacy, sex is the only way to do it.

The result of this ideology has been the *sexualization* of nearly every corner of our culture. Freedom of sexual expression is the mantra of our day, creating one of the most sexualized societies in history.

The pornography industry, for example, is an invisible economic juggernaut, bringing in more annual revenue than the NFL, NBA, and MLB combined. Though the precise numbers are difficult to calculate because of its heavy online presence, some estimates even have it generating more money than Microsoft, Google, Yahoo!, Amazon, and Apple *combined*.[33] The size, scope, and influence of sexual content are staggering. Research has found that 73 percent of women and 98 percent of men report viewing internet pornography in the last six months.[34]

This unceasing, aggressive pursuit of intimacy points to one obvious truth: people are searching for intimacy, but what they are finding isn't enough.

The themes of sex, pleasure, and relationships dominate the songs we sing, the movies we watch, and the stories we tell. Without question, we are searching, and sexual pleasure seems to be the quickest and easiest end of our search. Our culture's answer to the search for intimacy is *more sex*. Then more sex. Then more sex.

But is this thirst for sexual freedom actually setting anyone free? Now that people have easy access to sexual images and videos, and many casually participate in sexual acts, do we live in a society that appears satisfied? Are people content and fulfilled? Are they reporting higher levels of happiness? No. In fact, the opposite is true. It seems that the more you try to quiet your ache for intimacy with cheap sex and quick highs, the emptier and more isolated you become.

In 1 Corinthians 6, the apostle Paul dealt with the confusion around sex that was ransacking the church in the city of Corinth. At the time, the city was a booming economic hub, attracting thousands of young people from across the region. These young people were transient and far from home, and Corinth quickly became known as a place of sexual experimentation. At the center of the city was the famous temple of Aphrodite, where sexual experiences were seen as a form of worship. Cult prostitutes filled the streets of the city each night, and sexual experimentation was the accepted norm.

It was in this context that the church rapidly grew, but its new members were struggling to cut ties with their old ways. They wanted to live for Jesus, but they weren't sure how intimacy and sex were intended to interact. To make matters worse, the leaders of the Corinthian church were immature in their faith. It was a classic case of the blind leading the blind.

Remember in the Disney movie *The Little Mermaid* when the mermaid Ariel asks Scuttle the seagull to help her understand humans? She brings him a fork, and he tells her it's a *dingelhopper* used for combing hair. She brings him a pipe, and he calls it a *snarfblat* and says it makes music. The seagull has no idea how things are actually supposed to work! In the same way, the church leaders in Corinth didn't know their *dingelhopper* from their *snarfblat*, and things were quickly moving from bad to worse.

Paul began by dispelling some of the myths that the people were believing. They were claiming that, because Jesus had fulfilled the law, they no longer needed to obey God's moral commands. They saw sex simply as a physical appetite, like food for the stomach (1 Corinthians 6:12–20). Three times in this passage, Paul wrote, "Do you not know?" In other words, misinformation can have tragic consequences. If you aren't careful, your thirst for intimacy can lead you further away from what can actually satisfy your heart. He then introduced a critically important truth: "The body is not meant for sexual immorality, but for the Lord" (1 Corinthians 6:13).

What was Paul trying to tell us? God has a specific design for humanity. Just as a car runs on gasoline or a furnace runs on oil, God designed the human machine to run on *himself*. You can put diesel fuel in a gasoline engine for a little while and it will run. But it won't take long before the wrong fuel destroys the engine entirely. In the same way, the fundamental ache for intimacy in your heart cannot be satisfied with sexual pleasure, no matter how frequent. To try to satisfy your ache for intimacy with sex is to misunderstand your design. You can't run on diesel fuel. You need more than sex, and the implications of this error are devastating.

. . . .

To try to satisfy your ache for intimacy with sex is to misunderstand your design.

. . . .

Understanding Design

When Paul wrote that we are not meant for sexual immorality, he was saying something specific about God's design for sex. He quoted Genesis 2, where God placed one man and one woman in a garden and performed the first wedding ceremony.

God gave them sex as a bonding agent that would fuse the two together in a profound and mysterious way, so much so that the two actually *became* one. We see this bonding in the physical act of sex, where a man enters a woman and the lines between the two are blurred, but God's design goes much deeper. The act of sexual intimacy fuses the two together in every way—spiritually, emotionally, psychologically, economically, *and* physically.

Interestingly enough, science supports this biblical claim. During any sexual act, the brain releases dopamine to increase focus, norepinephrine to enhance memory, oxytocin to weld the emotional experience into the soul, and serotonin to create a sense of calm. The physical body uses every tool available to cause fusion.

Paul tells us that, in sex, two people are *joined*. The word he uses is actually a word that describes the process of welding, where two metals are joined together. One is heated to the point that it liquefies and intermingles with the other heated metal, until the two become one, creating an inseparable bond. Where one begins and the other ends is no longer discernible.

The discovery and use of fusion with metals are the foundation of our modern society. Bridges, skyscrapers, airplanes, and automobiles couldn't exist without the power of fusion. The ability to bond deeply creates the opportunity to build. In the same way, God designed sex for the covenant of marriage, as it fuses two people together in the act of sex, so that all of society could be built on the sturdy foundation of the family. This deep, exclusive bond brings stability to all facets of life.

But the connection was never intended to be strictly physical. It was designed to encompass the whole person. The husband and wife are emotionally bound together, spiritually bound together, and financially bound together. To ignore any level of the "one flesh" reality is to work against the inherent design. And this was Paul's primary concern with the Corinthian church. What happens to a person if God's design is ignored and a different ideology rules in its place?

When Paul tells us that the body is not meant for *sexual immorality*, he uses the Greek word *porneia*. This word refers to any sexual act outside the boundaries of a lifelong covenant of marriage between a man and a woman. Any sexual act outside those boundaries fights against God's design. Pornography falls into this category. Living with your boyfriend falls into this category. Masturbation falls into this category. To orgasm without your spouse is to rip the bonding gift out of the package of marriage.

So what is actually happening when a man watches a pornographic video? What is actually happening when a woman decides to sleep with her new boyfriend on the second date? What happens when people obey their natural impulses and experiment sexually outside of the marriage between a man and a woman?

In the physical realm, there is a flash of pleasure and then it's over. You may never see that person again. But in the invisible world, far more has taken place. *Fusion* has occurred. Two souls have mingled together. Oxytocin was released and norepinephrine wrote the experience in stone. You can shut the computer or walk away from the relationship, but whether you realize it or not, you have left something behind. You have lost a part of yourself.

Then it happens again, and again, and again. Our society promises that a little more sex will satisfy all needs. But despite all our sexual freedom, we are more depressed, anxious, and sexually unsatisfied than ever.

Is there a connection between the overarching sense of emptiness in society and the loose sexual expression that has become so common? Absolutely. Something tragic has occurred. With every sexual act outside of marriage, another piece of your personhood is forfeited. And the result? The fragmentation of personality. In an attempt to satisfy your ache for intimacy, you have lost your soul. And sexual sin plays for keeps.

Paul taught that sex in marriage is a gift from God but that it's not an end in itself. It's an arrow pointing to the final source. The body is *meant* for the Lord (1 Corinthians 6:13), and whoever is joined to the Lord becomes *one spirit* with him (1 Corinthians 6:17). Consider the implications behind this truth. Just as a man and a woman are fused together through the act of sex and the lines between where one begins and the other ends are blurred, so faith in Christ connects the Spirit of God to the spirit of man. The two are fused into one, and the lines between where God begins and man ends are blurred.

This is the gift of eternal life! It is the truest, deepest answer to your heart's cry for intimacy! And this is what Paul meant when he wrote, "'Therefore a man shall leave his father and mother and hold fast to his wife, and the two shall become one flesh.' This mystery is profound, and *I am saying that it refers to Christ and the church*" (Ephesians 5:31–32).

Do you see it? God wants to bring you back to the garden and walk with you in the cool of the day! He wants to marry you! No marriage can practically work if one party entertains other lovers, because the power of marriage is found in exclusivity.

This is why God outlines only two roads for the follower of Jesus and then promises to provide the power to walk down one of the roads. Either express the depth of Christ's love for the church through the covenant of monogamous marriage or express the breadth of true fulfillment in Christ through celibate singleness. Both roads honor God and redefine the cultural narrative around sex. Neither road will be traveled easily.

Boundary Lines

Living within boundaries is one of the most unpopular ideas in modern society. We live in an era where stretching the boundaries is celebrated and respecting the boundaries is mocked. If you are an athlete, the highest honor is to set a new record. If you are a scientist, the greatest accomplishment is to publish a new discovery. Just walk into the nearest gym, and you will find a passionate coach who is ready to help you set a new PR (personal record). We pride ourselves on going further, doing the impossible, and stretching the limits.

I remember, years ago, before I was married, I took my girlfriend out tubing on my uncle's boat. There we were, kids in love getting pulled on two water tubes at top speed. I wanted to impress her, so I shouted across the water, "I'm going to jump to your tube." She looked back at me terrified. I just smiled.

This was my moment—I was going to show her that I was the type of guy who stretched the boundaries in life. So I pushed off my tube, flew through the air, and landed next to her on her tube. In my mind, I had pictured the scene as a romantic moment where I wrapped my arm around her waist and she was taken aback by my strength and athleticism.

Instead, my arrival on her tube launched her into the air! Her body got tangled up between the tube and the rope and she was ripped into the water.

My uncle stopped the boat as my girlfriend resurfaced. Her earrings had been torn out of her ears. Her nose was bleeding and she had a black eye. She looked up at me and asked, "What were you thinking?"

Not all boundaries are meant to be broken. Sometimes, the bravest thing to do is to stay on your own tube. But this will fight against the impulses of our fractured nature. Everything in our culture is selling the myth that sexual boundaries are there to be broken and that more sex will fix your emptiness.

Therefore, if you wish to maintain the boundaries that God has etched into the universe, specifically in the area of sex, know that this won't be accomplished without extreme intentionality. And as soon as you commit your heart to follow one of the two roads God outlines for sexuality, you will discover that temptation is waiting around the next turn.

In Proverbs 7, we find a picture of how temptation works. The writer tells a story of a young man who flirts with a married woman. "Passing along the street near her corner, taking the road to her house in the twilight, in the evening, at the time of night and darkness" (Proverbs 7:8–9).

It always starts in the corners. This is where all temptation begins. The corner of your mind. The corner of your eye. When you entertain what's in the corners, temptation grows.

Imagine the scene. Maybe it's late at night and you've worked a long day. You get home, turn the TV on, and start flipping through the channels. Without your realizing it, the remote stops on a sex scene that's unfolding in a prime-time TV show. You start to feel the pull. Something is drawing you in. The temptation comes from the *corner* of your mind.

You realize that no one is home and your computer is right next to you. Your mind starts racing. The computer can open up a world of options, and there are plenty of other shows available on your television. This is where temptation starts: when the ideas in the corner of your mind are entertained.

The young man in Proverbs 7 seems to just be going for a stroll. He's tired, aimless, bored—it's late at night. Have you ever been there?

What happens next gives us further understanding of how temptation works.

> And behold, the woman meets him....
> She is loud and wayward ...
>> and at every corner she lies in wait.
> She seizes him and kisses him,
>> and with bold face she says to him,
> "I had to offer sacrifices,
>> and today I have paid my vows;
> so now I have come out to meet you,
>> to seek you eagerly, and I have found you.
> I have spread my couch with coverings,
>> colored linens from Egyptian linen;
> I have perfumed my bed with myrrh,
>> aloes, and cinnamon.
> Come, let us take our fill of love till morning;
>> let us delight ourselves with love.
> For my husband is not at home;
>> he has gone on a long journey." (Proverbs 7:10–19)

Do you see what's going on here? The woman begins by kissing him, sending a rush of chemicals through his brain. Then she talks about how she's a good girl, making vows to God. She can't possibly cause him harm. From there, she tells the young man that she's been looking for him. He is *wanted*. He is *valued*. She makes him feel like a man with the as-yet-unspoken promise to fulfill his deep desire for intimacy. She goes on to describe a sexual experience beyond his wildest dreams. She promises satisfaction, even telling him that she plans to make love to him all night long.

Finally, she gives him one more piece of information: her husband is gone. *No one will know.* There won't be any consequences or ramifications. You can watch that video, visit that website, hook up with that person, and keep it all a secret. The illusion is now complete, and the young man takes the bait. "All at once he follows her, as an ox goes to the slaughter ... [and] he does not know that it will cost him his life" (Proverbs 7:22–23).

This young man entertained the idea. He dabbled with the thought. Then he jumped in *all at once.* He goes for it, and he is described as an ox going to the slaughter.

If you're like me, you probably haven't slaughtered that many oxen. But in that day, this was a vivid picture that spoke directly to the common experience of the people. The ox would follow his owner. The animal was strong, powerful, and unassuming. The owner would hold the collar of the ox with one hand, then take a small, razor-sharp knife and quickly slit the ox's throat. The massive beast would collapse on the ground in shock, gasping for breath, and within minutes choke on its own blood.

The point of the passage is terrifyingly clear: to ignore God's boundaries is to wander into a slaughterhouse. And everyone who has entertained temptation and sinned sexually knows the flood of death that follows.

On the inside, shame and guilt swallow up your spiritual confidence. You can hardly pray without feeling suffocated under the shame. Your heart, once soft and aware of God's presence, now feels stone cold to the things of God. Your joy is gone. Your love is thin. You're easily frustrated at everyone and no one. Your entire spiritual relationship with God feels like a distant dream.

It's because you've been robbed. You left the front door open and sent an invitation to the thief to come by. "Do not be deceived ... for the one who sows to his own flesh will from the flesh reap corruption" (Galatians 6:7–8). You reap corruption—in your mind, your heart, and your emotions.

When it happens once, it breaks your heart. But it rarely happens only once. Pretty soon, you start to feel numb and you begin thinking that the only thing that can make you feel alive is another sexual experience. So the cycle continues, until any real relationship with God has been choked out, stolen, or forgotten.

I've seen it a thousand times. Soon, porn-addicted men or heart-trampled women begin finding excuses for why they are angry at the church, can't trust the leadership, or don't feel the Bible is relevant. All of these offenses are just symptoms of a deeper disease, which Paul would call corruption. They traded true intimacy for a lethal spiritual poison. And so often, the victim, like the ox, never saw it coming.

On the outside, there are great consequences too. Trust has been broken. People have been hurt. Hearts have been torn in two. Sometimes, the damage in relationships cannot be repaired. Sometimes, it leads to disease or unwanted pregnancy. All of this because you ignored the boundaries. They seemed archaic and unrealistic, yet in the end, less was more, and more was death.

God's boundaries are not intended to limit your life but widen it. Just as guard rails are placed along a highway to keep you safe and on track, God isn't looking to rob you or steal from you. Every limit he commands is for your benefit.

Scripture teaches at least four specific boundaries that must be embraced for the rediscovery of true intimacy.

Boundary 1: The boundary of a flawed soul. Jesus said that he blesses the poor in spirit by giving them the kingdom (Matthew 5:3). In other words, the first step toward freedom and victory is not choosing your own path but acknowledging your own brokenness. Sin has distorted the soul, and each of us is flawed and broken beyond repair, which means that you can't trust yourself in the area of sexuality and you can't figure out your own way. You can't *will* yourself into obedience.

You are not a good person who needs to be made better, or even a bad person who needs to be made good. According to Jesus, you are a dead person who can come alive only by his power (John 5:25). Brennan Manning famously wrote that "the spiritual life begins with the acceptance of our wounded self."[35] Paul wrote, "For I *know* that nothing good dwells in me, that is, in my flesh" (Romans 7:18).

. . . .

> You are not a good person who needs to be made better, or even a bad person who needs to be made good. According to Jesus, you are a dead person who can come alive only by his power (John 5:25).

. . . .

Do you know that about yourself? Do you know that apart from Christ you can never live sexually pure? Have you reached the boundary of your own ability and recognized the inherent flaw that your willpower cannot fix? Until you face the boundary of your own flawed soul, you will find yourself taking the bait of the adulteress again and again. Counterintuitively, the beginning of God's power is found at the end of yourself.

Boundary 2: The boundary of real accountability. Accountability is the direct acknowledgment to another person that you need help. In this context, accountability means finding a mature follower of Jesus of the same gender who is living in victory and inviting him or her into your mess.

First, confess to this person your areas of struggle with sexual sin. Don't be so vague that your accountability partner doesn't really even know what you're talking about. Be specific. It hurts, and it's embarrassing, but accountability brings healing (James 5:16). Then commit to talk regularly about your areas of weakness until you see habitual victory. Commit to reach out to your accountability partner *before* you give in to temptation. As soon as you are tempted, call him or her to break the spell. In this act of humility, God will respond by providing for you the power to walk away.

Boundary 3: The boundary of a future picture. In those moments of temptation, take the time to write out or think through this third boundary. Picture your life if you pushed the clock forward. What will be the result of following through on sexual temptation? What will life be like when it's over? How will it feel to sense that distance between you and God?

Consider the guilt, the shame, and the loss of spiritual confidence. Consider the vacuum of regret that will grow in your heart. Consider how the act will distort your view of intimacy, numb your spiritual sensitivity, and cloud your prayers. Consider how it will disqualify you from spiritual leadership and hurt the people around you. It will make you a worse parent, spouse, and friend. Think of the people your choices will hurt. It will destroy trust with those you love. How would it feel if others found out?

Remember the biblical story of Joseph? If he had given in and slept with Potiphar's wife, he could have easily been executed. Then who would have saved God's people from famine? His entire destiny could have been forfeited for a few minutes of pleasure! Or think about Samson. God intended him to be a great leader, but instead he died a blind prisoner. All because he wouldn't live within sexual boundaries.

Write out your thoughts. Use this third boundary to snap your heart out of the spell that sexual temptation casts.

Boundary 4: The boundary of resurrection power. Jesus didn't leave us helpless in the area of sexual temptation. He put his Spirit within us, giving us the power to say no when temptation knocks. The key to accessing that power is first understanding that you have it, and then believing that you can walk in it.

Romans 6 teaches that "we *know* that our old self was crucified with him in order that the body of sin might be brought to nothing, so that we would no longer be enslaved to sin" (Romans 6:6). Before you can overcome, you must know what is yours.

When Jesus died on the cross, God saw you in the death of his Son. This means that, in God's eyes, when Christ died, you died. Through your death, sin's power over you has come to an end. In the courtroom of heaven, sin's legal right over your life was canceled when Jesus paid your debt. When Christ rose again, you rose with him spiritually. Now, his resurrection life abides in you.

In order to experience the victory, you must *know* this truth and allow it to frame your point of view. "So you also must consider yourselves dead to sin and alive to God in Christ Jesus" (Romans 6:11).

If you don't *consider yourself* dead to sin, sin can still rule you like it did before you trusted Christ. The power to overcome temptation is accessed by faith. The more real this becomes to you, the more power you will experience. The four boundaries we've covered can point your life in this new direction and provide a framework for a new way of living.

So far we have looked at three critical habits that have the power to center your life around a relationship with God. But that relationship can run right off the road if guard rail habits are not in place. More than any other kind of sin, sexual sin can devastate your relationship with God. That is why habit 4 is so critical to your spiritual maturity and joy.

Habit 4: *Live within the accountability*
of biblical sexual boundaries.

As you start to develop the four boundaries outlined in this chapter, a new freedom will begin to emerge. You will experience a nearness to God that is not experienced any other way. The counterintuitive truth of sexual boundaries is that these limits don't actually limit you—they liberate! As you practice them, sexual boundaries will increase your joy and deepen your relationships.

But for many of us, the idea of sexual boundaries feels like too little too late. You may look at your story and think the damage has already been done. Maybe you've already welded your soul to various partners, images, and experiences. Maybe you're reading this right now and your heart is already numb. You've felt like the ox that walked blindly into the slaughterhouse.

If sexual sin is playing for keeps, then what hope is there for a fragmented, broken soul?

Is It Too Late?

The book of Hosea tells the story of a prophet whose life is ravaged by sexual sin. Hosea married a woman named Gomer, and after some time they had a son. Life was good, and the young family was thriving—until Gomer became pregnant with a second child, who was not fathered by Hosea.

This would crush any family, but Hosea didn't give up on their marriage. He named his illegitimate daughter Lo-ruhama, which means "you have not received mercy." Sometime later, the family received another blow as Gomer again got pregnant with another man's child. This time, God told Hosea to name the boy Lo-ammi, meaning "not mine" or "not of my people."

These two kids carried names that spoke of their mother's unfaithfulness. Every time their names were spoken, it was a reminder of her sin. Finally, Gomer gave up on the marriage and left Hosea, eventually selling herself into slavery. In a radical act of love and in obedience to God's command, Hosea searched for her, found her, bought her from the slave owners, and returned home with her.

It's an incredible story of redemption, and God included it in the Scripture because Gomer is a picture of you and me. You are the unfaithful wife, and God is the husband of your soul. Through acts of unfaithfulness, you have experienced the fragmentation of personality and found yourself enslaved by your desires. But in the greatest act of love, your husband came to find you. He sold all that he had to buy you back from sin and on the cross paid your ransom in full. Like

Gomer, you have been given more chances than you deserve, and even now God extends his hands in mercy.

Years after Hosea and Gomer, the apostle Peter wrote:

> But you are a chosen race, a royal priesthood, a holy nation, a people for his own possession, that you may proclaim the excellencies of him who called you out of darkness into his marvelous light. Once you were not a people, but now you are God's people; once you had not received mercy, but now you have received mercy. (1 Peter 2:9–10)

Peter teaches us that, because of what Jesus has done, there is a new identity for every believer, regardless of how ugly his or her past may be. This identity allows you to write a new script for your future.

He says you are *chosen*, answering the deep question "Am I valuable?" The answer is yes, because God chose you. You are *royalty*, answering the question "Am I significant?" The answer is yes, because God invites you to rule with him. You are a *holy nation*, answering the question "Am I part of something greater?" The answer is yes, because you are part of the kingdom of God. He calls you *his own possession*, answering the question "Do I belong?" The answer is yes, because you belong to him forever.

But what about the baggage of your past? What about the broken hearts, the dysfunctional relationships, and the memories that haunt you? After Gomer came back to Hosea, she still had her two illegitimate kids. The mistakes of yesterday don't just disappear when you repent. What does God do with yesterday's brokenness?

Did you notice that Peter included in his description of your new identity the names of Hosea's two illegitimate kids? Seemingly out of nowhere, Peter pulled their names back into the conversation. He wrote that you were once "not a people." That was the name of Hosea's son! You were once someone who had "not received mercy." That was the name of Hosea's daughter! The name over your past was changed from "not a people" to "God's people," and from "has not received mercy" to "has received mercy." God changed the name written over your past!

In Jesus, you have been given a new name. Peter pulled this tiny detail from an Old Testament story so you can know that it's not too late for you. God will change the name over your past sin, collect the broken pieces of your heart, rewrite the script of your life, and somehow turn shame into *glory*. He did it for Gomer. He did it for Peter. He can do it for you.

If you feel like habit 4 is out of reach, let me assure you that it's not. Take the first step toward healing and repentance and watch God transform you, day by day—from the inside out.

Father in heaven, I need your healing. I have acted outside the sexual boundaries you created for my benefit. I have trusted my desires over your word. Forgive me. Today, I turn to you and open my heart to your boundaries. Help me to take the next step into joy and freedom.

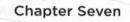

Chapter Seven

THE HABIT OF RESOURCES

Developing a lifestyle of generosity

"I am not commanding you, but I want to test the sincerity of your love by comparing it with the earnestness of others."

2 Corinthians 8:8 NIV

"I need a new outfit. There's nothing I can wear in this closet." Have those words ever come out of your mouth as you look through your options in the morning? My wife said something along those lines a few hours before the annual Christmas event at our church.

"What about this jacket?" I asked.

"I wore it last year."

"What about these jeans?"

"No, they won't work."

There's a huge closet full of clothes, and yet we are left with absolutely no options. Stunning.

For most of us, it doesn't take long before the new jacket feels old. It doesn't take long before the new thing begins to entice us.

Before you pass judgment on my wife, let me confess that I bought a new shirt for that Christmas event. I had to. I had nothing to wear.

I have only two feet, but I own far more than two shoes. I have sneakers for fun, sneakers for sports, and sneakers for the gym. I have dress boots, work boots, and work boots that I don't ever work in.

I have a friend who lived with only two outfits for over two years. Two pairs of shoes. Two shirts. That's quite an accomplishment in our world today. Many of us will wear more than that in a single day. Don't misunderstand me: I'm not trying to suggest that godly people should have only one pair of shoes. Rather, I'm suggesting that far too often we are unaware of the simple reality that, measured against almost any historical standard, whether you realize it or not, you are *rich*.

For most people in the West, being rich is a foreign and uncomfortable idea. We don't think we are rich. Rich people drive nicer cars than we do and live in bigger houses. Rich people have vacation homes in Italy and own a private jet. You're not *rich*. If, however, we take just a moment and zoom out from our own small glimpse of the world, the reality of our "richness" begins to sink in.

Do you own a car? The vast majority of the world's population does not. Do you have access to clean water? That puts you in a better position than 663 million people on the planet.[36] Do you make at least $20,000 a year? This may come as a shock: that puts you in the richest 4 percent of the world's population.[37] Do you make over $32,400 a year? You just landed in the richest 1 percent of people on planet Earth.[38] For most of us, this perspective is mind-blowing.

If you were born in an industrialized nation and had the money to purchase this book, chances are that you are rich by global standards. Millions of people on the planet are living by a very different standard. Your privileged position doesn't make you evil, but it does require a level of awareness and responsibility.

Paul gave some specific instruction for those who find themselves on the top of the financial pile in life:

> Command those who are rich in this present world not to be arrogant nor to put their hope in wealth, which is so uncertain, but to put their hope in God, who richly provides us with everything for our enjoyment. Command them to do good, to be rich in good deeds, and to be generous and willing to share. In this way they will lay up treasure for themselves as a firm foundation for the coming age, so that they may take hold of the life that is truly life. (1 Timothy 6:17–19 NIV)

According to the Scripture, wealth is not sin. Wealth comes with certain opportunities, but it also comes with certain dangers. Specifically, the danger of wealth is to become arrogant, trusting a mirage of self-sufficiency and putting your hope in your money. Paul was exposing for us a natural propensity of the heart that occurs in *all* of those who have means. Wealth provides a false salvation.

It's important to note that this doesn't happen to only some people with money. It happens to *every* person who lives with a degree of wealth. Money provides for the heart a sense of safety, security, and status.

When you have money, your heart will naturally become attached to it. Soon, you will feel more important because of your money. You will feel more in control of your life. Because you can afford that alarm system, or that door with a lock, or that backup savings account, you will feel safer. Without realizing it, your heart quickly creates an inner attachment to money. *Money makes me safe. Money helps me feel in control. Money makes me important.* This narrative has been building steam your entire life.

In Mark 10, Jesus challenged the rich young ruler to sell all that he had (Mark 10:17–23). Jesus didn't give this command to every person who wanted to follow him, but this young man's heart was trapped in an attachment to his things. After the rich young ruler left, unwilling to sell all that he had, Jesus followed up by saying, "How hard it is for the rich to enter the kingdom of God! … It is easier for a camel to go through the eye of a needle than for someone who is rich to enter the kingdom of God" (Mark 10:23, 25 NIV).

The analogy is clear: a camel will not fit through the eye of a needle—ever. Every single person with money is going to develop an unhealthy inner attachment to things. And you can't set yourself free. "With man this is *impossible*, but not with God; all things are possible with God" (Mark 10:27 NIV).

Whether we realize it or not, the security and status we find in money is a real problem for every follower of Jesus who comes from a culture of wealth. It requires that you examine your heart in ways you may not have considered and to fundamentally replace your concept of life.

A Concept of Life

What story or inner picture forms your perspective on the things you value? Whatever story you embrace, that is your concept of life.

For example, one of the most commonly held beliefs in our culture is that *life is like a race*. Whoever collects the most fame, notoriety, or success wins at the game of life. People spend their lives striving to be at the top of their fields or accumulate the maximum amount of money or status because, to them, life is a race.

Who are we racing against? It depends. Some of us race against our coworkers. Others race against our parents or siblings. Many people are racing against an invisible person, always living like they're a step behind but not entirely sure whom they are unable to catch. This "story" informs how you view everything you own. It's your concept of life. For the people who live by this story, every possession is a symbol of their position in the race of life.

Another common concept of life is that *life is like a party*. For people who embrace this mind-set, everything in life is leveraged to maximize comfort and pleasure. The more free time and recreation you have, the more successful you are. These people live for the weekend and do the bare minimum required to secure more time to party. This is their concept of life.

Still others embrace the notion that *life is like a great journey*. It's all about experiencing new things and traveling to new places. These people leverage their resources to secure new and unique experiences, traveling thousands of miles, or ending old relationships in the pursuit of something fresh and exciting.

You may have never thought of your life from a concept-of-life perspective. Maybe you aren't sure which story informs your point of view. For many of us, our concept of life changes depending on the day, month, or year. We often combine various ideas in search of greater fulfillment. John Eldredge rightly noted, "Most of us live in a fog. It's like life is a movie we arrived to 20 minutes late. You know something important seems to be going on. But we can't figure out the story. We don't know what part we're supposed to play or what the plot is."[39]

The story of the gospel cuts through the fog, outlining the greatest story of life and inviting us into it. Life, we are told, is ultimately about God. He is the main character in the movie, and we were created to display his glory. The role we are given is not the central role—that belongs to Jesus—but it is a crucial role. It is the job of every believer to take God's gift of life, along with the resources God provides, and *steward* those gifts to make much of him.

You were created to showcase his power and reveal his nature. So life is ultimately not a race, or a party, or a journey. *Life is a stewardship.* This is what the first story of Scripture reveals, when human beings are placed in a garden and instructed to "work it and take care of it" (Genesis 2:15 NIV). It's our job to steward God's creation. We don't own it; he does. But we have been given the sacred responsibility of managing what belongs to God.

In order for us to be good stewards, God must shake us out of our wealth-induced, entertainment-saturated fog and reveal to our hearts that, ultimately, we do not own anything. Everything belongs to him, and everything in our care must be seen as a stewardship. Your kids aren't yours. They are God's kids. Your breath isn't yours. That life belongs to God. And your money isn't yours. Not one dollar in your account. It all belongs to God. He's entrusted it to you to teach you responsibility, faith, and reliance on him. And he can take it away.

In my house, my three sons have all gone through stages where their Legos were the most important things on Earth to them. They've collected dresser drawers full of Legos, and each kid is pretty protective of his pile. One day, my youngest son, Ezra, decided to sneak into his older brothers' room and build an airplane out of the extra Legos in their dresser. When the older boys got home from school, Ezra started showing off his new plane. "Look at this plane I built. I made it myself. It's mine," he said with a toothless grin. The older boys recognized some of the pieces on the plane, and they knew he had raided their stash.

"Ez," they said, "you went into our room, took our Legos, rearranged their order, built a plane, and now you think it belongs to you? Just because you rearranged the pieces, it doesn't mean you own the plane."

It was a harsh reality for Ezra to face, but the older boys were right. And so is God. Just because you took the talents he gave you, the strength he gave you, the intelligence he gave you, and the opportunity he gave you, and made some wealth that comes from his creation—don't fool yourself into thinking that you are the owner. You're not. Everything—*everything*—belongs to him.

Has the concept of life as a stewardship rearranged the inner wiring of your heart? Has it transformed the way you look at your money? For most followers of Jesus, *stewardship* is a well-known Christian word, but it hasn't actually translated into a concept of life. And the results of that misstep are far-reaching.

God challenged his people through the prophet Haggai: "Now this is what the LORD Almighty says: 'Give careful thought to your ways. You have planted much, but harvested little. You eat, but never have enough. You drink, but never have your fill. You put on clothes, but are not warm. You earn wages, only to put them in a purse with holes in it'" (Haggai 1:5–6 NIV). Maybe you've felt this way—like you're always a dollar short or like you can never really catch up on your expenses.

God gives the reason behind the problem. "This is what the LORD Almighty says: 'Give careful thought to your ways.... You expected much, but see, it turned out to be little. What you brought home, I blew away. Why?' declares the LORD Almighty. 'Because of my house, which remains a ruin, while each of you is busy with your own house'" (Haggai 1:7, 9 NIV).

God tells us that these people made a critical mistake: they treated their stuff like it was ultimately theirs. They treated their money like they were the owners. And when money becomes your security, your source, and your safety, it's only a matter of time before God lets the wind blow and the house of cards comes crashing down.

So what are we supposed to do about our deep attachment to things? If 100 out of 100 of us naturally develop an unholy attachment to our wealth, and if nearly all of those who might read this book fall into the wealthiest 4 percent of the people on the planet, then how do we break free from this attachment? How do we live our lives fully attached to God rather than to things?

Open Heart Surgery

In his classic series *The Chronicles of Narnia*, C. S. Lewis introduced the unlovable character of Eustace Clarence Scrubb. Eustace is the cousin of the Pevensie siblings, who are the kings and queens of Narnia. If you're not familiar with the stories, you should know that these kids find a magical world beyond our own and leave life on Earth for adventures in the land of Narnia.

Eustace, however, is a selfish boy. He's cowardly and is almost always complaining. He gets dragged to Narnia with his cousins, and once he's in this magical land, he becomes obsessed with the treasure of a dragon. Eustace is warned to leave the treasure alone, but he can't resist. He aches for the wealth and power it would provide and eventually steals some of the treasure for himself. Because of his actions, Eustace comes under a spell and is transformed into a dragon himself.

At first, Eustace doesn't realize what's happening, but when he finally comes to the realization, he is tormented by the prison of his new body. Because he is now a dragon, everyone he approaches runs away from him, and everything he touches gets destroyed or catches fire. He has become a hazard to the world, and his new existence is a lonely one.

This story serves as a sobering picture of our hearts. As soon as you turn to wealth for security, status, or safety, a dragon heart begins to grow inside you. You will naturally want to cling to what you have, and then you will begin to build your sense of self-worth on your status or possessions. Eventually, the false salvation of money becomes so rooted on the inside that it weaves itself into your very identity. In your own mind, you can't separate who you are from what you own. In God's mind, you have become a dragon.

The story culminates when Eustace meets Aslan the Lion, who is a picture of Christ. Aslan finds Eustace trying to rip his dragon scales off, unable to remove the skin. Aslan finally tells him, "You have to let me do it."

Eustace describes what happens next:

> I was afraid of his claws, I can tell you, but I was pretty nearly desperate now. So I just lay flat down on my back to let him do it. The very first tear he made was so deep that I thought it had gone right into my heart. And when he began pulling the skin off, it hurt worse than anything I've ever felt.... Well, he peeled the beastly stuff right off.... And there was I smooth and soft as a peeled switch and smaller than I had been. Then he caught hold of me ... and threw me into the water ... and as soon as I started swimming and splashing I found that all the pain had gone.... And then I saw why. I'd turned into a boy again![40]

The problem of Eustace Clarence Scrubb is the same problem we face in regard to wealth: we can't set ourselves free. We can't break the spell. Jesus must do it. And the cure begins with the revelation of the gospel.

Back to the story of the rich young ruler: Right before Jesus challenged him to give up all he had, the Scripture describes one critical, often-overlooked fact. "And Jesus, looking at him, *loved him*" (Mark 10:21).

Before the young man had obeyed or disobeyed, before he had had the opportunity to trust, Jesus already loved him! The word used for "loved" in the text is the Greek word *agape*, which specifically refers to divine love. It is the perfect love of God that transcends reason, never wavers, and always calls with open arms. Before the young man's obedience, Jesus loved him! Do you see it?

The critical question that must be answered in order for your dragon heart to be changed is *"How does Jesus look at me?"* Does he look with eyes of disappointment? Does he look with eyes of disgust? Is he looking at you through the lens of an exacting accountant? Or a ruthless taskmaster?

The one truth that changes everything else is the truth that the posture of God's heart toward you, right now—*is love*! If this is true, then anything God asks you to do, he is not thinking of his glory only—he is also thinking of your good! All of his commands are for your benefit and blessing.

At its core, Christianity is not a list of rules to follow or sacrifices to make. Christianity is a radical change of heart caused by the profound revelation that you are loved by God! And the revelation of God's love reorders the priorities of the heart. When you are deeply convinced, through the evidence of the cross, that you are loved by God, the spell of money is broken and you can trust God with all that you have.

. . . .

Christianity is a radical change of heart caused by the profound revelation that you are loved by God!

. . . .

This powerful change of heart grows in us as the gospel takes root, and it is proven through a life of radical generosity.

Transformed Hearts Want to Give

In 2 Corinthians 8, the apostle Paul shared the story of the church of Macedonia. These Christians might be the most unlikely group of givers in all of Scripture. Paul was collecting a financial gift to take to the poor Jewish Christians in Jerusalem, and the Macedonians had no cultural connection with the Jews. As far as society was concerned, these two groups of people were on the opposite sides of the cultural spectrum: different languages, different traditions, different lifestyles.

On top of this, the Macedonians were brand-new Christians. They hadn't had much time to mature in their faith. To top it all off, the Macedonians were extremely poor. They barely had enough for themselves. It's in the middle of these circumstances that something supernatural happened.

> In the midst of a very severe trial, their overflowing joy and their extreme poverty welled up in rich generosity. For I testify that they gave as much as they were able, and even beyond their ability. Entirely on their own, they urgently pleaded with us for the

privilege of sharing in this service to the Lord's people.
(2 Corinthians 8:2–4 NIV)

These new Christians desperately wanted to give! Their hearts had been changed by the love of Christ, and the natural outworking of that change was the tangible giving of their money.

Paul stated it bluntly just a few verses later when he addressed the Corinthian church:

> But since you excel in everything—in faith, in speech, in knowledge, in complete earnestness and in the love we have kindled in you—see that you also excel in this grace of giving.
>
> I am not commanding you, but I want to *test the sincerity of your love* by comparing it with the earnestness of others. (2 Corinthians 8:7–8 NIV)

Consider the implications of what Paul wrote. First, he said that these Corinthian Christians were growing spiritually in their knowledge and passion, but they had some work to do in this area of money. After serving as pastor of a church for years, I can testify that for most of us, the last things to be born again in our lives are our wallets. The Corinthians had grown in a number of areas, but they hadn't learned the grace of giving. Paul didn't command them. Instead, he leveled with them. He said their generosity was an accurate test of the sincerity of their love.

Ouch.

In other words, the real evidence of genuine love is a generous life. You cannot claim to love God and then not practice radical generosity.

Why not? Because the purpose of God in the life of every believer is to make you more like himself. And God, at his very core and in the very essence of his nature, is not a *taker*. Unlike anyone else in the universe, God is purely and completely a *giver*! So God trains us to be givers like him by providing for our needs and then teaching us to let go of what we have in order that we may bless others with it. This cycle of receiving and then releasing teaches our hearts to mirror his heart.

When you follow God's principles of generosity, the spell of *money as my source* is broken and the revelation of *God as my source* takes root.

Paul outlined three principles of generosity that we can use to break the spell and reshape our hearts in God's image.

My Top Priority

When Paul explained the incredible heart change that had occurred among the Macedonian Christians, he wrote, "They gave themselves first of all to the Lord, and then by the will of God also to us" (2 Corinthians 8:5 NIV).

This is the first big step of faith that every believer must take if we want to mature in love. We must give *first*. Before you pay your mortgage, before you buy your groceries, before you save for retirement—you set aside money to give. In the eyes of our world, this concept sounds ludicrous. Giving can't take precedence over food on the table—can it?

God teaches our hearts to trust him by commanding us to give first (Matthew 6:33). When I give last, after all my bills are paid and my needs are met, there is no faith involved in the transaction. But when I give first, before any of my needs are met, I am making a declaration to the world and to my own heart. My actions proclaim that *God is my source, God is my safety, and God is my provider!*

Have you ever walked up to a vending machine, starving, only to see a sign that reads "Out of Order" hanging on the glass? What does that phrase really tell us? In our culture, it simply means that something is broken, but in actuality, the statement reveals more. To be out of order means that one or more of the steps in any given system is functioning out of its intended position. When something is designed to happen third, but it starts happening first, the system fails.

Like a vending machine, our hearts operate on a system that requires a specific order. God can be real in your life only to the degree that he is first in your life.

Some people wrongly assume that, because God is God, he can do anything he wants—but there are some things that even God can't do. For example, God cannot lie. He is perfect truth. Also, God cannot change. It is impossible for him to improve, decline, or learn.

In the same way, God cannot be second. Theologians call this his *preeminence*. He is ruler of all, creator of all, sustainer of all. God is always first. To make God second in your heart is in direct contradiction to his essence. You cannot connect to him until you approach him as he truly is: *first* in everything. The Macedonian Christians gave themselves first to God, and this led to their radical generosity toward others.

Years ago, I heard a preacher tell the story about a rancher and his wife. The rancher had a cow that was pregnant, and when the cow finally had her calf, to the rancher's delight, she had twins. The rancher had been planning on selling the calf and making a great profit, and now his return would be double. He ran inside to tell his wife. "Honey, the Lord has blessed us richly! Rather than having one calf, we have two! We are so blessed by God, when I go to the market and sell both these calves, I want to give half of what we make to the church."

"Wow," his wife replied. "That is so generous."

"Well, God has blessed us so much," the rancher said.

Time went by, and one day the rancher came in from work with a sad look on his face. "What's wrong?" asked his wife.

"Oh, honey, it was a sad day today. The Lord's calf died."

"What do you mean?" asked his wife. "I don't remember ever designating one of the calves as the Lord's."

"Oh, yes," said the rancher. "Since they were born, I knew which one would be ours to sell and which one would be the Lord's. Unfortunately, we won't be able to give that money to the church since the Lord's calf died."

If we're honest, it's always the Lord's calf that dies.

When God isn't first in our giving, the first thing to go when times get tough is our generosity. But if we will trust God by giving first, we will discover that he takes full responsibility for the life that is completely yielded to him (Luke 18:29–30). In this way, we deeply learn to transfer our trust from our money to our God. He becomes in our hearts the Lord who provides!

The principle of giving first has rightly been called *priority giving*: generosity is my first financial priority.

Finding Generous

After Paul described the heart of generosity displayed by the Macedonian church, he challenged the Corinthians to trust God through giving as much as the Macedonians had done.

> Now finish the work, so that your eager willingness to do it may be matched by your completion of it, *according to your means*. For if the willingness is there, the gift is acceptable *according to what one has*, not

according to what one does not have. (2 Corinthians
8:11–12 NIV)

After teaching them priority giving, Paul here outlined the second
critical principle of generosity: *generosity looks different for every person.*
Jesus illustrated this truth when he noticed a woman in the temple giving
her last two copper coins (Luke 21:1–4). He told his disciples that she
had given more than all the rich people had, because she had given all
she had to live on. Jesus didn't stop her from giving—even in her poverty.

Sometimes we mistakenly think that poor people shouldn't give,
but this is not what Scripture teaches. Every person, regardless of our
wealth, should give to the work of God on Earth because it's through
giving that we develop a heart like God's heart. "Each of you should
give," Paul later wrote (2 Corinthians 9:7 NIV). This means that every
Christian, regardless of wealth, should be a giver.

In the book of Acts, a man named Ananias (not the same Ananias
whom God used to help Paul) sold a piece of property and gave some
of the proceeds to the church. At first glance, this looked radically
generous, but Ananias had lied about the amount that he had sold the
property for. He pretended to give all the money from the sale, when
in fact he had given only a portion of the profits. Ananias wanted to
look generous without feeling the effects of real sacrifice, and God cut
his life short for his deception (Acts 5:1–11).

These two stories illustrate the principle of proportionality. We
each must give in proportion to what we have. The stories warn us not
to judge the seemingly small gift of one person, because to that person
it may be a great sacrifice, and not to be impressed with the seemingly
big gift that may have cost someone very little. Generosity is an issue
of the heart.

Each person must wrestle with the question "How much would I have to give in order to detach my heart from trusting in things and attach my heart fully to God?" For many of us, that's a scary question. The Old Testament gives us a starting place by teaching the practice of tithing. Tithing is one of the more debated topics in Christianity. Biblically, tithing is giving 10 percent of your income back to the work of God, and in the New Testament era and beyond, the tithe goes to the local church.

. . . .

Each person must wrestle with the question "How much would I have to give in order to detach my heart from trusting in things and attach my heart fully to God?"

. . . .

A brief study of the Old Testament finds that Abraham tithed, and so did his descendants. Moses included tithing in the Old Testament Law. And Jesus later affirmed the practice of tithing (Matthew 23:23). God spoke through the prophet Malachi and told God's people that to withhold the tithe was to rob God, but giving the tithe would unlock unprecedented blessing (Malachi 3:8–10).

Many people today emphasize the point that tithing is not explicitly commanded in the New Testament. That's true. It's strange, however, to receive the kindness of God through the sacrifice of his Son and then respond by doing less than the Old Testament law commands. Everything in the New Testament points to Christians expressing greater generosity, not lesser.

But the blessing of tithing is most clearly seen in the evidence of real life. After tithing for over twenty years myself and talking to hundreds of people who also do it, I have never met a tither who doesn't share the same story: "God made a way! It didn't add up, and it was scary at times, but God made a way and we are more blessed for giving than we would have been if we'd held on to what we had."

Giving 10 percent of your income back to the work of God is a powerful step of faith. The idea of a specific percentage is so helpful because it allows each of us to give according to our means. This principle has been called *percentage giving*: you set aside a specific percentage of your income to give.

Grow in Your Grace

After Paul taught the Corinthians about priority giving and percentage giving, he moved on to the third critical principle of generosity:

> Remember this: Whoever sows sparingly will also reap sparingly, and whoever sows generously will also reap generously.... And God is able to bless you abundantly, so that in all things at all times, having all that you need, you will abound in every good work. (2 Corinthians 9:6, 8 NIV)

He started by telling them to *remember*. Why did he write this? Because it's easy for us to forget. The natural mind assumes that, if you give something away, you will have less for yourself. It seems painfully obvious. If you give a dollar, it no longer is yours. If you don't give the dollar, it remains yours. Simple. But Paul was revealing the deeper principle that our natural minds often miss.

Because God is teaching your heart to be generous like his heart, he treats your money like a seed. Every farmer knows that the seed that stays in your hand does you no good. In order to receive a harvest, the farmer has to let go of the seed. Functionally, he loses control. The seed is in the ground. But it is under the earth where growth must take place. The seed sprouts into a plant, produces a crop, and generates thousands of seeds to replace the one that was sown.

This sentiment was powerfully captured in the book of Proverbs when the author wrote, "The world of the generous gets larger and larger; the world of the stingy gets smaller and smaller. The one who blesses others is abundantly blessed; those who help others are helped" (Proverbs 11:24–25 THE MESSAGE).

Paul was not teaching that we should give so that we can get. That's the wrong motive for generosity. We should give simply for the joy of giving—to become more like God and to reflect his image. But the truth remains: it is actually more blessed to give than to receive (Acts 20:35).

When you give much, God reciprocates by giving much back to you. Does it always return in the same form you gave it? No. Does a seed look like the plant it produces? Not really. Giving money away doesn't always mean you'll get money back—but it does mean you'll receive *life*. Life is, of course, the point after all—and it may come in the form of inner peace, deeper joy, greater opportunity, or financial benefit. However it comes, those who sow finances will receive an abundance of life in return (2 Corinthians 9:8).

Paul's promise to generous people is stunning. He made it clear that your surplus will always exceed your sacrifice. But you have to trust. You have to step out. You have to embrace being uncomfortable and losing that sense of control.

There are functionally only two ways to live when it comes to our money. We can operate from a scarcity mentality, or we can learn to develop an abundance mentality.

Scarcity thinking comes naturally to all of us. It asks, "What about me? I'm afraid I won't have enough. If I give, I will have less." An abundance mentality flows from a deep conviction of the love of God. It says, "I have a Father in heaven! He takes responsibility for me and is my provider! He has promised to supply more than enough for his kids, and when I give, he trusts me with more."

Scarcity is rooted in fear. It still views my things as my source. Abundance is rooted and grounded in love. It views God as my source. The only way we learn to grow in abundance thinking is by stretching the boundaries of our generosity year after year. This principle is called *progressive giving*. I continue to increase my giving over time.

With these principles outlined, you are ready to incorporate habit 5 into your life.

Habit 5: *Structure your life around priority,*
percentage, and progressive giving.

Notice that habit 5 requires that you structure your life around these principles. That means that the implications of this habit stretch beyond just your money. It will impact who you choose to marry. Does he or she uphold these same values? It will impact what career you choose and what house you buy. Structuring your life around giving means intentionally reflecting on your values and then moving things around as necessary. This process should be incredibly invasive, and at times very painful. Our hearts don't release control without a fight.

Augustine, one of the early church fathers, taught extensively on the idea of what he called *disordered loves*. He wrote that a good person "is also a person who has [rightly] ordered his love, so that he does not love what it is wrong to love, or fail to love what should be loved, or love too much what should be loved less (or love too little what should be loved more)."[41] Ordering our loves rightly brings freedom, joy, and abundance, but there is a deep and undeniable connection between what our hearts love and how we spend our money.

This is why Jesus said that "where your treasure is, *there* your heart will be also" (Matthew 6:21). The affections of your heart will always follow your greatest investment. Invest your very best in the stock market, and you'll find yourself checking the status of your stocks constantly. Invest your best in your kids' education, and it will be primary in your heart. Invest your first and best in God's kingdom—and your heart will follow.

Augustine taught his church to pray a simple but powerful prayer: *"Set love in order in me."*

Are you willing to allow God to reorder the loves in your heart? Are you ready to grow in the grace of giving? Are you ready to give in a way that forces your heart to rely on God as your provider?

Father, you promise to provide for your children. But I have this tendency to cling to what I have. My heart forgets that I am the steward, not the owner. Set love in order in me. Stretch me. Make me a giver, like you. I choose right now to take the next step in the grace of giving. Guide me. Teach me to rely on you fully as the Lord who provides.

PART 4: LONG HAUL LIVING

"Every scene in a movie is moving toward a final scene.... I need to determine what kind of final scene I want and then develop a plot that gets me there."[42]

Lance Witt

"After twenty-five years of priesthood, I found myself praying poorly, living somewhat isolated from other people, and very much preoccupied with burning issues. Everyone was saying that I was doing really well, but something inside me was telling me that my success was putting my own soul in danger."[43]

Henri Nouwen

"Emotional deficits are manifested primarily by a pervasive lack of awareness."[44]

Peter Scazzero

 Chapter Eight

THE HABIT OF RHYTHM

The ongoing practice of Sabbath rest

"So then, there remains a Sabbath rest for the people of God, for whoever has entered God's rest has also rested from his works as God did from his."
Hebrews 4:9–10

It's been said that breakdowns often lead to breakthroughs. I have found it to be true in my life.

This time, I honestly didn't see it coming, and that might be the most embarrassing part, because the writing wasn't just on the wall—it was everywhere. It was on the faces of my wife and kids. It was in the concerned looks from my friends. But I was operating from a profound lack of self-awareness, and I didn't seriously consider drastic change until the room was spinning. Literally.

I fondly refer to the day of my undoing as my Dunkin' Meltdown. But before we get to the climax, I'll give you some of the backstory.

When I was twenty-eight, blessed with a wife and three kids, I set out to start a church in the least-churched region of the United States.

To everyone's surprise, including my own, the church grew quickly. What had started with nine friends rapidly became a larger community. We added new staff and new locations. God was profoundly blessing our efforts.

I told my wife that, to really get things off the ground, it would take three brutal years of sacrifice—three years of hard work, long hours, and a grueling schedule. We agreed that starting something like this came with a cost, and so we set out in faith, willing to sacrifice, willing to burn the candle at both ends for three years.

But the three years passed, and my warp-speed pace turned out to be not a temporary burst but my new way of life. So three years became four, then five.

I got pretty good at keeping everyone happy while still moving at lightning speed. I made time to date my wife and attend my kids' sports games. I was a noble martyr, doing my best to never rip off the people around me. I didn't skimp on my times of prayer, my sermon prep, or my family time.

But to live this way for that long, I had to rob someone—so I just kept robbing my own soul.

It started with physical symptoms. I didn't *feel* particularly stressed, and I didn't feel emotionally or spiritually empty, but I had these random, rotating physical ailments. For a month or two, it would be chest pain. Then dry patches under my eyes. Then ringing in my ears. It felt like every year I'd pick up two or three nagging physical issues, until one night I ran into an issue that I couldn't ignore.

I was lying in bed at 11:00 p.m., and though my mind wasn't racing and my body was tired, I just couldn't sleep. Soon, it was midnight. Then four in the morning. Still no sleep.

I got out of bed the next day having dozed off for a couple of minutes, but for the first time in my life, my body just wouldn't turn off. I prayed about it. I cast out every demon I could think of. But nothing helped.

The same thing repeated itself the next night. And the next. Night after night, I'd just lie in bed—not feeling stressed in my mind but still unable to fall asleep. This went on for a week, then two.

In week number four of almost no sleep, I was driving to the office with a massive cup of coffee from a nearby Dunkin'. Theirs isn't my favorite cup of coffee, but I was just trying to survive at this point.

Without sleep, life gets pretty weird. Things you've taken for granted your entire life are now in jeopardy, and an overall sense of helplessness creeps in. Ironically, in the midst of this, I honestly never slowed down and considered that my sleep problem might be evidence of a deeper issue. The morning of my Dunkin' Meltdown, I pulled into the parking lot at the church and jumped out of the car as if nothing was wrong, preparing for another buzzing day of work.

And then it happened.

I couldn't walk. I could hardly see. The parking lot started moving ... then spinning. I got back into my car, afraid that someone on staff would see me staggering around. Alone, I put my hands on the steering wheel to steady myself, and the floodgates opened. I started to cry. I had officially lost control. I was melting down, and it had snuck up on me like a ghost.

I called my good friend Rog and told him everything. He didn't mince words. "Justin, you are living life at an unsustainable pace. If you want to move forward, you have to completely change the way you live. You have to allow God to teach you a new rhythm."

A new rhythm? At the time, I couldn't see anything that needed to change. I was fully devoted to Jesus. I was living for the mission. I was spending an hour with God every morning, sharing my faith every week, following the leading of the Spirit, living in sexual purity, and giving my money generously.

True, I had no hobbies and no leisure time. I had very few mentors speaking into my life. I was out with church work multiple evenings every week. I never exercised. I ate garbage. And I had no understanding or commitment to a life that included a Sabbath rest.

Without realizing it, I had fully embraced one of the great American virtues. I'm not referring to the virtue of liberty or innovation. I am referring to the great American virtue of *ceaseless activity*. It's the perspective that says bigger is better, faster is better—more is better. Why would you ever order regular size when there's super-size? As a culture, we wear ceaseless activity like a badge of honor.

Just the other day, I went with my son's Boy Scout troop to meet the mayor of a nearby town. He explained to the kids all the important things he was responsible for in his position. One of the boys raised his hand to ask a question. "Mr. Mayor, how much do you work?"

The mayor leaned forward and cracked a smile. "Son," he said, "as the mayor of this town, I work seven days a week, twenty-four hours a day, 365 days a year." I watched as looks of admiration grew on the faces of these little boys, each of them internalizing the lesson: *important people never stop.*

In fact, ceaseless activity is no longer up for debate in Western civilization. It is simply *what is.* Americans work longer hours, take less vacation, and retire later in life than anyone on Earth. But when most Americans hear these statistics, we don't shrink back in shame. Instead, we sit up a little straighter and puff out our chests. "Sleep when you're dead," we say under our breath.

I had to learn from experience that if you don't sleep you will be dead pretty soon.

What is all this ceaseless activity producing in our lives? *Stress.* That's the word we use to describe the overtaxing of our physical, emotional, and psychological reserves. Not surprisingly, 77 percent of Americans report experiencing physical symptoms caused by stress. Seventy-three percent report suffering from stress-induced psychological symptoms. Forty-eight percent of people in the US report lying in bed at night, unable to sleep![45] Looks like I'm not completely crazy after all—or at least, I'm not alone.

Why are we killing ourselves with ceaseless activity? What are we chasing? What are we so fixated on? For many of us, the answer is actually simple: our eyes are fixed on The Scoreboard.

What is The Scoreboard? It's the invisible tracking system that proves your worth and value in the world. It tells you if you're some-body. The Scoreboard exists in nearly every area of life, and we've learned as a society to remain aware of the score in every moment.

It exists in your marriage—when you keep track of how many sacrifices you've made versus how many your spouse has made. It exists with your friends—when you compare the intelligence and accomplishments of your kids with those of their kids. It exists in the office—when you pull into the parking lot and look at the cars, comparing them to your own. The Scoreboard rules social media, when you scroll through pictures of someone else's vacation or special moment. It's the reason you secretly rejoice when that other person is overweight. It's the reason you relish the idea of your project growing while someone else's project fails.

The Scoreboard tells you where you fit in the world. It has economic categories, physical beauty categories, achievement categories, and intelligence categories. And if you stop—if you disengage—everyone else will run ahead of you. And you will know once and for all that you don't measure up.

The Scoreboard flexes its power most in the areas of your deepest insecurity. It thrives on the need to be approved of. It whispers to your soul, convincing you that you must prove yourself *again*.

Tragically, many of us are living oblivious to its influence. We are deeply unaware of how much it controls our lives. Pastor Peter Scazzero called this hidden part of yourself your *shadow*:

> Everyone has a shadow. So what is it? Your shadow is the accumulation of untamed emotions, less-than-pure motives and thoughts that, while largely unconscious, strongly influence and shape your behaviors. It is the damaged but mostly hidden version of who you are.[46]

In previous generations, people found significance primarily through the agency of the family. You were important because you were somebody's daughter, somebody's brother, or somebody's dad. In our time, however, this concept has faded, being replaced by The Scoreboard. Today, significance in life comes primarily through deciding what you want out of life and attaining it. Without realizing it, most of us are living in the tyranny of performance, forever trying to prove ourselves through ceaseless activity.

Do you know what the Scripture calls a life like this? *Wickedness*. To live this way is evil. "But the wicked are like the tossing sea, which cannot rest, whose waves cast up mire and mud. 'There is no peace,' says my God, 'for the wicked'" (Isaiah 57:20–21 NIV).

How do we break out of this wicked cycle? How do we cut ties with our cultural expectations? It's not going to be easy.

Leaving Egypt

The book of Exodus in the Old Testament tells the story of God's people and their miraculous liberation from the most powerful empire on Earth. The people of Israel were slaves in Egypt and, for four hundred years, never had a single day off. Each morning, God's people would wake up, collect straw, and make bricks. Day after day, generation after generation.

Through their years of oppression, the people of God internalized a lesson: *you exist to produce.* Your value and worth are directly connected to your performance—and if you do not produce, you have no reason to exist.

Sound familiar?

Through a series of miracles, God set his people free from slavery in Egypt. Now, they were a new nation not yet arrived at their homeland, and God gave them a gift.

> Six days you shall labor and do all your work, but the seventh day is a sabbath to the LORD your God. On it you shall not do any work, neither you, nor your son or daughter, nor your male or female servant, nor your animals, nor any foreigner residing in your towns. For in six days the LORD made the heavens and the earth, the sea, and all that is in them, but he rested on the

seventh day. Therefore, the LORD blessed the Sabbath
day and made it holy. (Exodus 20:9–11 NIV)

The word *Sabbath* comes from the Hebrew word *Shabbat*. It literally means "to cease, to stop." The word can also be translated "to
celebrate." This is the dual essence of the Sabbath. God told his people
that, on one day out of seven, he wants them to completely stop. Don't
labor. Don't push any of your goals forward. Just stop and celebrate.
The rest of the Old Testament records for us how God's people struggled to obey the Sabbath command, revealing just how difficult this
requirement really is.

Although God's people had left Egypt, the Bible seems to indicate
that Egypt hadn't left them.

It turns out that stopping one's activity takes more intentionality
and discipline than not stopping. In fact, by the time Jesus walked the
earth, the religious leaders of the day had somehow turned Sabbath
into a performance of its own. They had added dozens of regulations
to the Sabbath: don't remove a stain from your clothes on the Sabbath;
don't change the water in your flower vase on the Sabbath. The list goes
on and on.

Jesus appeared to intentionally walk all over their extra rules. They
were furious when he healed a man on the Sabbath and when his disciples plucked grain from the field. To these religious leaders, following
the rules of the Sabbath positioned a person in right standing with
God. Somehow, Egypt had once again stolen their rest. Their mantra?
Your value is connected to your performance.

We look at these silly rules of the Pharisees and turn up our noses at
them. How could they be so foolish? Yet this perspective of *performance*

equals acceptance has so deeply altered our gospel message that grace is often unrecognizable.

For many of us, the gospel has been turned into performance. Jesus died for our sins because he loves us, so we'd better live good lives and be good Christians if we want Jesus to welcome us into heaven. Do you want to hear, "Well done, good and faithful servant"? Well, you'd better spend an hour every morning in prayer and share your faith every week. You'd better tithe and never look at porn.

Without even realizing it, we take grace and turn it into law. We fall back into a performance mind-set as our default. You do this, and so do I. The Scoreboard is still casting a shadow over your conscience. But the real secret to a life of rest can be discovered only through the blessing of the Sabbath.

The Lord of the Sabbath

In Luke 6, the religious leaders were once again furious with Jesus because of his lack of rule-keeping on the Sabbath. Jesus addressed his critics multiple times before he finally threw down his ace: "The Son of Man is lord of the Sabbath" (Luke 6:5).

What did he mean by that? By the way, he was referring to himself when he said "the Son of Man," as this was the prophetic name given to the Messiah in the book of Daniel. Jesus was trying to reframe their understanding of the practice of Sabbath. The day of rest was given to God's people as a physical reminder of a deeper spiritual truth: you don't need physical rest only—you also need soul rest. You can sleep for ten hours and still wake up with a weary soul. You don't need a break from physical work only—you also need the peace and inner rest that come from perfect acceptance before God.

But how can anyone attain that? As a sinful person, your conscience is never on sure footing before the holiness of God. And that was why Jesus called himself the lord of the Sabbath. He was saying, "All the regulations point to me! All the traditions point to me! I am *your* Sabbath rest."

God tells us this prophetically in the book of Exodus. "Say to the Israelites, 'You must observe my Sabbaths. This will be a *sign* between me and you for the generations to come, so you may *know* that I am the LORD, who *makes you holy*" (Exodus 31:13 NIV).

Do you see it? The Sabbath is a sign. And what does a sign do? It points to a destination. The practice of Sabbath as physical rest points to God's promise of deeper soul rest for his people. This rest can be obtained only when we realize that we cannot make ourselves holy. God makes us holy through the death of Christ on the cross. Jesus received our restlessness, writhing in agony on the cross, so that we could receive his perfect record of righteousness before a holy God. He makes you holy!

This is why the book of Hebrews tells us, "So then, there remains a Sabbath rest for the people of God, for whoever has entered God's rest has also rested from his works as God did from his" (Hebrews 4:9–10). Christ is your Sabbath rest! But you must enter into him. You must see yourself *in Christ*. You must abide in him as a branch abides in a vine (John 15).

Remember when God gave Israel the Sabbath command? He gave them a reason for the command—and the reason wasn't "because you really need a day off." Rather, he told them that God himself had worked for six days but on the seventh day, he'd rested. The justification for our Sabbath is God's rhythm.

Why would God rest? Was he tired? Was he worn out from all that galaxy building? Of course not. God has never been tired. He didn't rest because he was tired; he rested because he was *satisfied*—and that distinction makes all the difference.

So how do you find true inner rest? You find it by realizing that, when God looks at you, he sees your life through the lens of his Son. And because of the cross, God sees you and is deeply *satisfied* with you. You don't have to prove yourself. You don't have to perform. In the eyes of the one whose opinion matters most, you are his *beloved*. This is the true Sabbath. This is how you take down The Scoreboard. No more posturing, no more proving. You are loved by God.

· ·

Because of the cross, God sees you and is deeply *satisfied* with you.

· ·

Brennan Manning put it this way:

> Living in awareness of our belovedness is the axis around which the Christian life revolves. Being the beloved is our identity, the core of our existence. It is not merely a lofty thought, an inspiring idea, or one name among many. It is the name by which God knows us and the way He relates to us.[47]

Henri Nouwen stated it plainly: "Being the Beloved constitutes the core truth of our existence."[48]

Do you remember on which day in the creation story God created man? It was on the sixth day. So Adam's first full day of life on Earth was the seventh day. Imagine the scene. Adam opens his eyes for the first time and drinks in the beauty of the garden. He is overwhelmed by all he sees, and his deepest joy is having intimate interaction with God. Adam falls asleep in the arms of his Father that first night and wakes up ready to go.

"What will we do today?" he asks God. "Should I build a house? Till the soil? Should I clear away this brush?"

"No," says God. "Today, you should rest with me."

God works, and then he rests, but man must first *find* rest. Begin from a place of rest in God, and then work *from* rest rather than *for* rest. This is the real secret to fully living. And here is where the practice of Sabbath comes full circle. The essence of Sabbath is fulfilled through Christ. More than anything else, you need soul rest, and that is found when you see yourself in him.

But how does the truth of the gospel really take root in your heart? How do you *know*, not just intellectually, but experientially, that you are the beloved? God uses the weekly routine of Sabbath to write on your heart the truth of the gospel. Without this intentional time and space, the love of God will be only a theory in your life. In order for your heart to internalize who you are in him, you must take time weekly to pause, pray, and play. You must physically stop and be replenished. You must create a weekly space in your schedule.

Remember what God said about the Sabbath in Exodus 20? He told us that he *blessed the day*! The actual day of rest is blessed. He doesn't specify which day; he simply says one day in seven. When you create the habit of resting one day out of every seven, there is a unique blessing from God and a unique internalization of the gospel.

The Invitation

What will it take to live in the Sabbath rest that Jesus offers your soul? What will it take to actually experience the peace that surpasses all understanding? It will require that you declare war on the cultural pressure toward ceaseless activity. You will have to radically adjust your plans. And yes, this may cause you to fall behind the productivity of your coworkers and friends. You may look irresponsible or even foolish.

Jesus extends to every believer an invitation into a different way of life. "Come to me, all you who are weary and burdened, and I will give you rest. Take my yoke upon you and learn from me, for I am gentle and humble in heart, and you will find rest for your souls. For my yoke is easy and my burden is light" (Matthew 11:28–30 NIV).

He offers us his yoke. In ancient times, a yoke was a piece of wood that connected two plow animals together. It meant that everywhere one of the pair went, the other went with him.

Notice that Jesus does not offer to take *your* yoke. He's not a genie that grants your every wish. Finding rest requires that you take his yoke. You go at his speed. You follow where he leads. Jesus says that, if you do take his yoke upon you, the results will be astounding. Because sharing the yoke of Jesus means that he's inviting you into a joint destiny. Where he is, you will go. What he obtains, you will obtain. The reward that awaits him, you will likewise receive.

It will require that you learn from him. This means an entirely different pace of life. It means incorporating the weekly rhythm of Sabbath into your routine. Not as a religious law, but as a spiritual strategy to free yourself from a performance culture and break the power of a performance mentality in your own heart. What is the weekly practice of Sabbath for the believer in Jesus? Biblically, Sabbath is a twenty-four-hour block of time in which we stop work, enjoy rest, and delight in and contemplate God. This leads us to habit 6.

Habit 6: *Practice living by grace through a weekly Sabbath routine.*

Every week, designate a twenty-four-hour period and mark this as Sabbath time. To do this weekly is an act of faith. It's a way of telling your soul, "This world can run without me. I am not God. I do not keep the planet spinning on its axis."

. . . .

Natural reason says, "If I leave that undone, I'll fall behind." But supernatural reason says, "By leaving that undone, I am declaring my trust in a God who works while I rest."

. . . .

If you do this, things will be left undone and projects will go uncompleted. That's why Sabbath takes faith. When you walk away from that unfinished project, you are submitting your life to a reason greater than your own. Natural reason says, "If I leave that undone, I'll fall behind." But supernatural reason says, "By leaving that undone, I am declaring my trust in a God who works while I rest. He is the Captain of my soul, and I am dependent on him." This act of faith releases the blessing of the Sabbath. Wayne Muller said it this way:

Sabbath is not dependent upon our readiness to stop. We do not stop when we are finished. We do not stop when we complete our phone calls, finish our project, get through this stack of messages, or get out this report that is due tomorrow. We stop because it is time to stop.[49]

The practice of Sabbath is also an act of liberation. It is your way of declaring war on a system that would try to convince you that you are what you produce. Don't misunderstand: your work *is* important, but it is not the deepest part of who you are. Every time you engage in Sabbath, you suffocate the power of your own insecurity. You break the curse of shame, stepping into Christ and out of striving.

The need to perform and prove yourself has been chasing God's people ever since they were making bricks in Egypt. To get Egypt out of you, you must break the cycle through weekly Sabbath.

Creating a Rhythm

Once we have internalized the power and potential of Sabbath-keeping, it's time to actually create a plan for Sabbath. What do you practically do? Is Sabbath simply a day off? Is it a day to run errands, pay bills, and clean the house?

Though it is unwise to create rigid, legalistic laws for your Sabbath day, Sabbath works best if running errands and paying bills happen during a different time of the week. The twenty-four-hour period called Sabbath should, as much as possible, revolve around three activities: pause, pray, and play.

After my Dunkin' Meltdown, Sabbath-keeping became one of my new disciplines. Things didn't change for me overnight, and I still have a lot to learn, but with the Dunkin' Meltdown now a few years in the rearview mirror, I'm beginning to see how much self-awareness I've lacked. My friend Rog was right: I needed to develop an entirely new way of living.

For me, this included a monthly meeting with a spiritual director—a pastor much older than me who could help me process things in my own soul. I learned more about Sabbath practices and healthy rhythms through reading books like *The Emotionally Healthy Leader* and *Replenish*, among others.

Further, I invited a group of older men into my life to regularly ask me difficult questions and look for chinks in my armor. I started exercising five days a week. I started eating in healthier ways. I cut back my work hours significantly. For the first time in my adult life, I made time for myself—time for hobbies and fun. I stopped working most evenings. Maybe most important of all, I began experimenting with the discipline of a weekly Sabbath, figuring out what replenishes me physically, spiritually, and emotionally.

Today, I hardly recognize the dizzy man staggering around the church parking lot with a huge cup of coffee in his hands. I know I'm not nearly out of the woods. But I'm starting to see beyond the trees.

These three Sabbath practices set the tone for twenty-four hours of renewal:

Pause. Sabbath is a day to stop. This means something different for every person, but stopping should feel a bit uncomfortable. Dallas Willard described it like this: "Accept the grace of doing nothing. Stay with it until you stop jerking and squirming."[50] If you're like me, inactivity feels very unnatural. I'm a doer, so not having a plan and not moving ahead take some getting used to.

In the Old Testament, the people of Israel were instructed to give their land a Sabbath rest every seven years (Leviticus 25:1–7). They were told not to plant anything but to just let whatever comes up to grow. This is a powerful picture for our understanding of Sabbath. This day should include some unscripted time—that's time when you don't have a plan and you don't know what you will do. Instead, you allow whatever is growing to grow.

Is it a sunny day? Maybe you go for an unplanned walk. Is it a rainy day? Maybe you spontaneously start a new book. Your soul needs space in order to be healthy, so some of Sabbath must simply be a *pause*. On my Sabbath, I am not checking email. I am not surfing social media. Instead, I'm just letting the day come.

If that feels like pure torture at first, then you're probably on the right track. After a little while of your squirming and resisting, the waters of your soul will begin to calm, and the inner voice of God will get clearer.

Pray. Sabbath is a special day to commune with God. It's a day when you can walk outside the lines of your normal morning prayer routine. It's a good day to review everything you've read or studied throughout the week. It's a good day to deeply contemplate the works of a great Christian writer. It's a good day to put on your favorite worship songs and lose yourself for a while.

One of the great truths that is often forgotten in our world is what theologians call *divine immanence*. It simply means that God is close right now. Sabbath is a time to remember the nearness of God. It's during these times of prayer on Sabbath that God preaches to us the story of our identity. He convinces your soul that you are *his*. He makes the truth of the gospel flesh and blood in your life. Sabbath is a time to meditate on the truth that you are loved and accepted—not because of what you do, but because of what Christ has done.

Play. Sabbath should include fun. Fun looks different for every person, but having fun on Sabbath is an act of faith. It's enjoying the gift of life even though things are still undone in your world.

What is fun for you? Maybe it's playing a sport or gathering friends for a board game with cups of good coffee. Maybe it's spending time with people you love, taking a trip to your favorite restaurant, or spending a night out to catch a movie. Sabbath shouldn't be all play, but it also shouldn't lack some good time for fun.

This area has probably been the hardest for me. When I started this practice, I honestly didn't know what I enjoyed. It's taken me years to discover what I like to do for fun, and it's been an amazing gift from God.

Doing Sabbath well takes intentionality and planning. Thinking through your upcoming Sabbath day and marking out time to pause, pray, and play will not happen unless you are incredibly intentional. You may feel guilty, unproductive, or wasteful. You may feel anxious or uptight for a while. But soon the blessing of Sabbath will begin to feed your soul and inject life into every other day of your week.

It's strange that God has to command us to rest and enjoy life, and still we resist. But he speaks a powerful promise for every person who steps out in faith.

> "If you keep your feet from breaking the Sabbath
>   and from doing as you please on my holy day,
> if you call the Sabbath a delight
>   and the LORD's holy day honorable,
> and if you honor it by not going your own way
>   and not doing as you please or speaking idle words,

> then you will find your joy in the LORD,
>   and I will cause you to ride in triumph on the
>   heights of the land
>   and to feast on the inheritance of your father
>   Jacob."
>   For the mouth of the LORD has spoken. (Isaiah
>   58:13–14 NIV)

God doesn't want you to do whatever you want on a day off. He also doesn't want you to work 24/7. He wants you to take one day a week to pause, pray, and play. Through this practice, you will find your joy *in him*. He will teach you to ride in triumph on the heights of the land and to feast on your inheritance.

The implications of Sabbath are so far-reaching that we have only scratched the surface in this chapter. It's time for you to go deeper and make some real changes—to rearrange everything, if necessary, and to discover the diamonds hidden in the Sabbath day. What will you stop doing? What will you begin doing right now?

Father, I have deeply internalized the false virtue of ceaseless activity. Forgive me. Right now, I repent. I commit to a life of Sabbath-keeping. Help me not to turn this gift into a law. Help me to learn from Jesus, the Lord of the Sabbath. Write the truth of your grace and my belovedness deep within my heart.

Chapter Nine

THE HABIT OF REPLICATION

Leading others in a process of discipleship

"So, being affectionately desirous of you, we were ready to share with you not only the gospel of God but also our own selves, because you had become very dear to us."

1 Thessalonians 2:8

The message of Jesus was never intended to be safe. They killed him after all, and they killed his closest friends. When the gospel message takes root in your life, it is nothing short of revolutionary. It's not a helpful add-on to your already busy life. No, the message of Jesus changes everything.

Dietrich Bonhoeffer said it best when he wrote, "The cross is laid on every Christian. The first Christ-suffering which every man must experience is the call to abandon the attachments of this world.... When Christ calls a man, he bids him come and die."[51]

Die to your plan. Die to your way. Surrender. Entrust your life wholly to God. And make the pursuit of him the center of your life. This is the essence of discipleship.

But as soon as you decide to do this—as soon as you take the step and trust God with your whole heart—you will discover that saying *yes* to being a disciple on the one hand and *living out* the call of discipleship on the other are two very different things.

Shortly before writing this, I came downstairs to find my ten-year-old son, Noah, drawing a picture. He loves to draw, so it's not uncommon for him to sit at the table for hours working on his art. But on this particular day, he had tears welling up in his eyes. I noticed the smudges of graphite up his arm and the eraser dust all over the table. "What's wrong, buddy?"

"Dad, I can't draw a dog."

"Yes, you can," I told him. "You're a great artist."

"No! I've tried like a hundred times. It looks like a cow or a horse. I can't make it look like a dog without looking at a picture."

Noah was spending all his time erasing and re-erasing because he needed a picture. Not just an idea in his head. Not just a description with words. He needed to see the dog if he was going to re-create one.

My son was feeling the tension that every disciple of Jesus feels at one time or another. We know that Jesus is our example and that being a disciple means learning to think, act, and live like him. Scripture tells us to fix our eyes on Jesus (Hebrews 12:2) and to follow in his steps (1 Peter 2:21), but even with the account of his life in Scripture and the guidance of the Holy Spirit, every disciple of Jesus longs for something else. We want to *see* discipleship lived out and practiced in our context. We want to walk with someone, observe how the person lives, and learn from what we see.

We want a picture.

The cliché that a picture is worth a thousand words may never have been more true than in the area of discipleship. How do I know that

I'm reading the Bible correctly? How do I learn to pray in a way that God answers? What does it look like to share my faith with a family member? What does it look like to have a godly marriage? How do I live for Christ while I'm single? How should I handle the struggle of poverty or blessing of abundance? What should I do when everyone else at work is cutting corners?

As Johnny Cash famously said, "Flesh and blood needs flesh and blood."[52] We want to see life correctly lived out. The Greek philosopher Epictetus said it this way: "We all carry the seeds of greatness within us, but we need an image as a point of focus in order that they may sprout."[53]

Likewise, while Jesus is our ultimate model, his plan for discipleship works only in the context of flesh-and-blood training. We all learn best by observing others who live out the gospel in front of us.

On June 7, 1944, the day after D-Day, American soldiers scrambled to survive the German counterattacks. In his book *Citizen Soldiers*, Stephen Ambrose retold the story:

> Brigadier General Norman "Dutch" Cota, assistant division commander of the 29th Infantry, came upon a group of infantry pinned down by some Germans in a farmhouse. He asked the captain in command why his men were making no effort to take the building. "Sir, the Germans are in there, shooting at us," the captain replied. "Well, I'll tell you what, Captain," said Cota, unbuckling two grenades from his jacket. "You and your men start shooting at them. I'll take a squad of men, and you and your men watch carefully. I'll show you how to take a house with Germans in it."

Cota led his squad around a hedge to get as close as possible to the house. Suddenly, he gave a whoop and raced forward, the squad following, yelling like wild men. As they tossed grenades into the windows, Cota and another man kicked in the front door, tossed a couple of grenades inside, waited for the explosions, then dashed into the house. The surviving Germans inside were streaming out the back door, running for their lives.

Cota returned to the captain. "You've seen how to take a house," said the general, still out of breath. "Do you understand? Do you know how to do it now?"

"Yes, sir."[54]

The captain's hesitancies and insecurities dissolved as soon as he saw a picture. It's this type of training that every follower of Christ longs for. We need to practically learn how to take a house, and God's plan to teach us will always require other people. When we actually see discipleship lived out, our rate of spiritual growth multiplies.

Growth by Association

How did Jesus take the gospel message from the dusty streets of Galilee to a worldwide movement? He didn't leverage the power of social media. He didn't find high-capacity investors to launch a global brand. In fact, the New Testament accounts of Jesus are painfully thin on training materials. He left his disciples with very few overt systems to implement. Why? Because he understood something about spiritual revolution that we tend to forget quickly: it doesn't fly on the back of programs—it's carried in the soul of *people*. This is the central core of Jesus's plan to change the world. Changed people *change* people.

Consider the absurdity of his plan from our postmodern, global perspective. Jesus lived thirty years in relative obscurity, then spent three years of ministry, living every day with twelve devoted men. These twelve men were his plans A, B, and Z. If they failed, no one would remember the name of Jesus. No one would know the way of salvation! Jesus risked *everything*—the entire salvation of humanity—on twelve less-than-impressive men. And his plan worked! It worked so well that the message of the gospel has crossed every ocean and reached every continent. Billions of people call on his name every day. And Jesus entrusted it all to the Twelve. This is nothing short of breathtaking.

In a classic work on the discipleship methods of Jesus, Dr. Robert E. Coleman wrote,

> His concern was not with programs to reach the multitudes, but with men whom the multitudes would follow.... It is not better methods, but better men and women who know their Redeemer from personal experience—men and women who see his vision and feel his passion for the world—men and women who are willing to be nothing so that he might be everything—men and women who want only for Christ to produce his life in and through them according to his own good pleasure. This finally is the way the Master planned for his objective to be realized on the Earth, and where it is carried through by his strategy, the gates of hell cannot prevail against the evangelization of the world.[55]

In his letter to the church in Philippi, the apostle Paul encouraged the leaders of the church with these words: "What you have *learned* and *received* and *heard* and *seen* in me—practice these things, and the God of peace will be with you" (Philippians 4:9).

Notice how many things Paul listed. He didn't say, "Listen, church, just take my letters and do what they say." Paul knew that that was not the strategy of Jesus. Instead, real discipleship happens through flesh-and-blood training. He told them to remember what he had taught them but also to remember what they had seen and heard from him. How did Paul handle his free time? What kind of horse did he ride in on? Was it a mustang or a bronco? Everything about his life was a lesson in following Jesus.

Beyond this, they *received* certain things from him spiritually. He prayed for them and released God's blessing over them. And all of this was part of transferring the message. It was growth by association. So much of the Christian life must be caught rather than taught, and that is exactly what Jesus intended.

In the introduction, I told you about the night in Chicago when I felt God challenge me to learn how to make disciples. After I came home, I quickly realized what I needed more than anything was a picture or model.

It was right around this time that I met Shawn, who was leading a ministry a few hours north of where I lived. We met at a large Christian music event and hit it off right away. It didn't take long for Shawn to invite me and a few of my friends to his house to meet some of the other guys in his ministry, and what I encountered when I got there blew my mind. We pulled onto the property and cars were parked everywhere. They were double-parked in the driveway and parked up on the grass. *Looks like they're having a party*, I thought. Turns out, this was just another ordinary day in their world.

When we walked in, my eyes were drawn to the largest dining room table I had ever seen in a house. It could probably have seated twenty-five people. Shawn's wife, Stephanie, greeted us and started introducing their five kids. But then someone else came up from downstairs and another person walked in from the backyard. Soon, people were everywhere, every one of them seeming as if they owned the place.

What I learned later about Shawn was that God had given him a vision for a community house. They had ten or so people living at this large property, along with two more properties full of people down the street. They called it *intentional community*. Functionally, it was a bunch of Christians living in close proximity for the purpose of frequent interaction and deep spiritual growth.

For all the craziness that ensued, I saw something at Shawn's house that carried the fragrance of Jesus. Isn't this what Jesus did? Living with his disciples, eating together—doing life together? It's true that actually moving in with ten other Christians is an unrealistic expectation for many of us, but is it possible to capture the essence of intentional community in your current stage of life? What would it look like for you to live with a greater emphasis on spiritually focused relationships?

I came home and started my freshman year in college with a desire to experiment. How could I maximize my own spiritual growth? How could I challenge others to really live a life of discipleship?

By my sophomore year in college, I had moved into a dorm room with three new Christians and had the real-life opportunity to try out intentional community. We would pray together. We would share our faith together. We would talk about Jesus in the midst of everyday activities.

It took two years to grow out of the dorm room, and by my senior year in college, I had moved off campus with three other guys. We rented an apartment with the specific vision of making disciples. As new guys met Jesus, they would often move in with us. We eventually got up to nine guys in our two-bedroom apartment!

After graduation, I got married, but the experiments with intentional community had only just begun. My wife and I bought a multi-family house and invited a few people to live with us (not always a great idea for newlyweds). Then our best friends bought a house near ours. We had eight people in our house, and they had nine in theirs. Every week, we would spontaneously get together for cookouts or times of worship. Those days were sweet, filled with deep conversation and friendship.

It was during this time that I first came across John Wesley's questions for small groups. Wesley had led a spiritual revolution in the 1700s across Europe, and the fuel behind the fire was intentional community. Small groups would gather in what was initially called "a holy club" and engage in honest conversation about the conditions of their spiritual lives. They would ask each other questions like "Am I consciously or unconsciously creating the impression that I am better than I really am?"; "Did the Bible live in me today?"; and "When did I last speak to someone about my faith?"

These questions were formative for my thoughts on functional discipleship. It was during that time that the six habits outlined so far in this book began to take shape. But we needed to go further.

Seven years into our experiment, my wife and I bought a second house down the road from our multi-family house. Our best friends bought the house next door, and other friends bought the house behind ours and then the house on the other side. Within a few years, we had ten or so houses full of people doing life together. We had no financial backer; we were individually buying mostly fixer-upper houses in the city.

But something supernatural was happening. A fire had started. There were spontaneous times of gathering and worship throughout the week. People were talking about Jesus while we pushed our kids on the swings or played Wiffle ball. The gospel had officially broken out of our church and invaded every moment of our lives. One minute we'd be cooking hot dogs; the next minute we'd be praying together. We were learning the Jesus way of discipleship.

You may be reading this right now thinking that there's no way you're joining a Christian commune. Please understand: I'm not at all suggesting that you do so. You don't need to sell your house or buy houses on the same block as all your Christian friends. Rather, you need to create a plan that allows other followers of Jesus to have regular access into your life for the intentional purpose of spiritual growth and accountability.

You have to find a way to do this. It will look different for you. But real discipleship can't happen until we increase the proximity between ourselves and others who are also in pursuit of God.

Discipleship must be a hands-on, life-on-life, flesh-and-blood, learn-by-association endeavor. People are not widgets. True disciples cannot be produced on an assembly line. They are forged in the fires of authentic relationship. You may never live with twenty people or buy a huge dining room table. But you have to find a way to create a discipleship environment in your context and stage of life, and it will definitely require moving out of the safe bubble of individualism.

. . . .

Discipleship must be a hands-on, life-on-life, flesh-and-blood, learn-by-association endeavor.

. . . .

This type of discipleship takes time—lots of time. Time to gather, time to hang out, and time to just let relationship breathe. Then it takes people engaging one another around spiritual issues. This will sometimes violate the boundaries of personal autonomy. It requires that you are deeply *known*—the good side, the ugly side, and the unfinished corners.

Intentional community works best when it finds its way into the margin moments of life. It might look like going grocery shopping with a friend and discussing your relationship with God while you're walking the aisles. It might look like making room in your house for a small group to gather every Tuesday night. The truth we must face is that rapid spiritual growth cannot happen until you combine frequent proximity with spiritual intentionality.

This style of discipleship requires a small group of people. The *Two Pizza Rule* is a good test. As soon as you need more than two pizzas to feed the group, it probably should split and become two groups.

It will require vulnerability—and that's dangerous. People often get hurt when they get this close. Just ask Jesus himself. Peter denied him, Thomas doubted him, and Judas betrayed him. But even with all the heartache that is often involved, flesh-and-blood training is still exponentially, counterintuitively effective.

Dr. Coleman concluded that "a few people so dedicated in time will shake the world for God. Victory is never won by the multitudes."[56] Growth by association is the front door to Jesus's discipleship plan. Gather a group of spiritually hungry people. Stay in close proximity. Gather often—and gather with the goal of becoming like Christ.

· ·

Gather a group of spiritually hungry people. Stay in close proximity. Gather often— and gather with the goal of becoming like Christ.

· ·

Pastor Wayne Cordeiro famously said, "You can teach what you know, but you reproduce what you are."[57] This is the secret of true discipleship. The only way to reproduce the life of Christ in you is to give people access to who you *really* are.

The tragedy of postmodern Christianity is that far too often we are busy with Bible studies, church activities, and community service, but we neglect the intentional process of discipleship. We often do this because we don't have a clear road map to make disciples. What should we do first? What should we do second? This book is intended to serve as that road map.

What if you began to walk alongside a younger Christian, teaching him or her the first habit of relationship with God? After some growth, what if you then guided that person through the second habit? Brick by brick, the person you're walking with would begin to grow. And *your* spiritual growth would also rapidly accelerate as you passed on what you've learned.

This brings us to our seventh and final habit.

Habit 7: *Build an intentional circle of discipleship.*

What if you started a small group that focused on deeply, intentionally applying these habits? Your circle might begin with just one other person. That's fine. It might have three or four. Start with habit 1, then work through each of the habits together. In the sections below, I will outline what it might look like if you did put together such a group. How exciting this would be!

The Process

A deep spiritual relationship will never grow until you dedicate time to it consistently. Begin by setting a regular time to meet. Will you gather every Monday at 6:00 a.m. before work? Will you gather once a month on a Saturday? As you start meeting regularly, take time to learn each other's stories. How did you become a follower of Jesus? What changes have occurred in your heart and life since deciding to follow Christ? How are you growing in your pursuit of God?

Once your small group gets to know one another, a natural leader will emerge. Who seems to initiate spiritual growth? Who appears to hold the deepest trust of the group? Are the other people willing to follow his or her lead? Jesus brought his group together, and Peter naturally rose to the top. Give the natural leader permission to initiate, and keep each gathering focused on growth.

Together, jump right in with habit 1: *spend the first hour of your morning alone with God.* If this feels overwhelming, start with fifteen minutes, then move to thirty. Gather and discuss what you did during your time with God and what God spoke to you.

Don't wait until you perfectly execute habit 1 before moving to habit 2. Once your small group has some traction in a habit, it's time to introduce the next one.

In habit 2, begin by making a list of five people in your life who are far from God, and commit to pray for them every day. Then challenge one another to pick the most difficult person on each of your lists and initiate a spiritual conversation with him or her. Come back together later and discuss how things went. Move through all six of the previous habits over the course of a number of months. It may take years before there's real traction among your members. That's okay. The goal is progress, not perfection.

The day will come when your group's spiritual growth can't move forward until some decisive action is taken, and it's the responsibility of the leader, along with the rest of the group, to challenge each person to *act* on what you discuss. For one person in the group, it might mean finally talking to his or her dad about Christ. It might mean finally being honest about that porn addiction. Each participant in the group should ask, "What do I need to do to apply what we discussed to my life?" That one question will keep any small group from feeling stale or irrelevant.

Any call to action from your group should not be manipulative or controlling, but it should be compelling, motivated by love. If a person is unwilling to act or just not ready to act, the group should be patient and supportive. But eventually those unwilling to act will be left behind as others grow and mature. This is an area where a pastor or other leader from your local church can serve as a catalyst to challenge those who seem stuck in their spiritual growth. Stay closely connected to the leadership in your church, and God will continue to push your group to new levels of maturity.

Imagine this discipleship process playing out with you and two of your friends. You gather every Friday morning, talk about your spiritual lives, and challenge one another. At first, you learn to spend daily time with God and hear his voice. Then you begin sharing your faith. You talk about money, sexual purity, and healthy life rhythms. Everyone in the group is experiencing profound and rapid change.

This progress shows that it's time for the next level: you have to find someone less spiritually mature than you and give away what you've learned. God has fashioned the human heart in such a way that information becomes revelation as it is passed on from one person to another. In other words, it's not enough just to have your band of brothers. You must guide someone else who is new to faith into spiritual maturity.

Which leads us to a sobering question: *Looking over your life, how many people have you actually discipled?*

Can you think of five people? Or three? Can you think of one? I've asked this question to hundreds of mature Christians, and the responses reveal a significant blind spot in our thinking. Tragically, many Christians have followed Christ for many years and can't remember a single person they have really, intentionally guided to a place of spiritual maturity.

Maybe you're a great worship leader or small group leader, or maybe you serve your church in another way. Maybe you volunteer every Sunday. All of these things are wonderful. But didn't Jesus command us to make disciples? Doesn't disciple-making need to be a part of every Christian's life? It's time for all of us to become disciple-makers.

The Anatomy of a Disciple-Maker

The apostle Paul modeled the heart behind successful discipleship when he wrote to the church of Thessalonica. He began by telling the church, "For our appeal does not spring from error or impurity or any attempt to deceive, but just as we have been approved by God to be entrusted with the gospel, so we speak, not to please man, but to please God who tests our hearts" (1 Thessalonians 2:3–4).

Notice that Paul intentionally *appealed* to them. He shared a compelling vision of what life could be like as a follower of Christ. He told them about a life full of joy, a life of peace with God, a life brimming with hope, power, and purpose. If you are going to make disciples, it begins with an appeal. Look for those who already display a hunger for God and are eager to grow. Don't ever drag someone into discipleship—it will never work! Find someone who is spiritually hungry, and appeal to him or her that life can be different.

After Paul appealed to the Thessalonians with a greater vision, he immediately dealt with *motive*. He bared his heart before them, telling the church plainly that he had no intention to manipulate or deceive. He emphasized the fact that he was not a man-pleaser.

> But just as we have been approved by God to be entrusted with the gospel, so we speak, not to please man, but to please God who tests our hearts. For we never came with words of flattery, as you know, nor with a pretext for greed—God is witness. (1 Thessalonians 2:4–5)

Impure motives will sabotage the discipleship process. If you care more about people liking you than you do honoring God, you can never make disciples. Paul lived to please God, which purified his motives. He didn't take advantage of people or push his agenda on them. His only motive was to help them grow—not hit a quota or feel important.

"Nor did we seek glory from people, whether from you or from others, though we could have made demands as apostles of Christ"

(1 Thessalonians 2:6). Once Paul had appealed to these Christians with vision and demonstrated a pure motive, he modeled an attitude of deep humility.

Discipleship can never be tainted with a controlling, domineering spirit. In fact, the word *disciple* literally means "learner," and it's from this attitude that the leader must lead.

Leadership in God's kingdom is not about telling other people what to do. It's about serving others for their joy.

"But we were gentle among you, like a nursing mother taking care of her own children" (1 Thessalonians 2:7). As an expert disciple-maker, Paul was casting vision, clarifying motive, and taking a humble posture, but then he quickly introduced *family* language.

The point Paul was trying to make is that discipleship works only through the framework of family. A family sticks together through the good and the bad. A family loves, even when you're a little crazy. A family forgives often and learns from one another. No one is above admitting that they are wrong. This is the heartbeat of healthy discipleship.

I remember a time years ago, when I was first introduced to a new person at our church. He had recently surrendered his life to Christ and was making huge leaps of growth in his faith. I shook his hand and asked him his name. "My friends call me Caesar, but my family calls me Damian." I smiled at him and said, "Great to meet you, Damian." It stuck, and virtually no one calls him Caesar to this day. He was certainly our friend, but more importantly, he was family.

Jesus taught that the family of God is a deeper, longer-lasting connection than even our blood family (Matthew 12:48–50). This family framework should profoundly influence the way you lead. We don't give up on people when their lives fall off the rails. We forgive again and again. We tolerate one another's annoying tendencies, and in the process, we learn to love like family.

"So, being affectionately desirous of you, we were ready to share with you not only the gospel of God but also our own selves, because you had become very dear to us" (1 Thessalonians 2:8). This is my favorite part of the entire passage. It's so honest and compelling. Paul told his disciples that his commitment to them went far beyond communicating a message. His commitment was dangerous. He was risking his heart because he had given his disciples his very *self*.

You simply can't make disciples without putting your heart on the line, because discipleship is not just passing along helpful lessons. In order to effectively make disciples, you have to let yourself care, which means becoming vulnerable.

"For you remember, brothers, our labor and toil: we worked night and day, that we might not be a burden to any of you, while we proclaimed to you the gospel of God. You are witnesses, and God also, how holy and righteous and blameless was our conduct toward you believers" (1 Thessalonians 2:9–10).

Paul didn't just teach these people; he also worked himself into a sweat, and he let them see it. He lived in a holy way when it looked like no one was watching. If you got close to Paul, you wouldn't find a cheap facade full of good slogans but little substance. You would see a man who lived what he believed.

There is nothing more compelling in life than a man who lives what he professes in the unseen moments of life. It's no wonder Paul left a vast congregation of disciples in his wake.

"For you know how, like a father with his children, we exhorted each one of you and encouraged you and charged you to walk in a manner worthy of God, who calls you into his own kingdom and glory" (1 Thessalonians 2:11–12). Paul was always encouraging, and he always believed the best in his disciples, but that didn't stop him from challenging them. His discipleship had teeth. He dealt with tough issues head-on. He *charged* them to walk in a manner worthy of God. He created a sense of accountability.

This passage of Scripture is a beautiful picture of healthy discipleship. Paul ended with this thought: "For what is our *hope* or *joy* or *crown* of boasting before our Lord Jesus at his coming? Is it not you? For *you are our glory* and joy" (1 Thessalonians 2:19–20).

Paul told us that there is no joy quite like the joy of seeing someone you've invested in really grow. Making disciples is an invitation into a whole different level of living, because your highest joy in life is found in the growth of another.

Have you been missing out on the joy of discipleship? Have you been living an individualistic Christianity, where no one has access to your interior life? Now is the time for change. Now is the time to find one other person and begin an intentional process of spiritual growth.

Start with habit 1. Discuss it. Apply it. Then move to habit 2. Before you know it, you and your small circle of friends will see rapid spiritual change. As you reach habit 7 together, the cycle repeats itself. Pretty soon, hundreds of changed lives will result from the intentional choice to start one small circle of discipleship.

Jesus, use me to make disciples. I want to effectively lead others in their spiritual growth. I want to be someone worth following. Today, I commit to the process. Take me to the next level.

PRACTICAL THOUGHTS FOR TOMORROW MORNING

"But the goal of our instruction is love from a pure heart and a good conscience and a sincere faith."

1 Timothy 1:5 NASB

What is Christian maturity? What does it really mean to be a mature disciple of Christ? If you can quote the Bible inside and out, does that make you spiritually mature? If you participate in every activity at church and are always the first to volunteer, does that make you mature? If you perfectly perform the seven habits outlined in this book down to the finest detail, does that make you a mature follower of Jesus?

The essence of spiritual maturity has been a frequent topic among Christians for generations. We often create long lists and come up with exhaustive categories to try to get our heads around the idea of what it means to be a mature disciple.

Before he was known as America's greatest theologian and a key leader in revival, Jonathan Edwards sat in his dorm room as a college student and wrote a list of over seventy *resolutions*. They described the life he intended to live, and they are compelling, dealing with issues like godly character, time management, and money. I first found these resolutions in the formative stages of my ideas around Christian maturity, and they lit a fire in my heart. Some of them have become foundational pieces in the bedrock of my life. Here are two:

Resolution 6: *Resolved, to live with all my might, while I do live.*

Resolution 7: *Resolved, never to do anything, which I should be afraid to do, if it were the last hour of my life.*[58]

These resolutions have had a profound impact on me personally, but with over seventy resolutions, the essence of Christian maturity still seems a little difficult to grasp. It wasn't until years later that Edwards boiled down Christian maturity to one single word: *love.*

"The only mark of genuine spiritual maturity and ministry effectiveness," Edwards concluded, "is the outworking of *agape*—a self-giving love for God and others. That is the one quality of our lives and leadership the devil can never counterfeit."[59]

Love. Not natural love, but supernatural love. Not simply the love of a brother or a spouse, but something deeper. This *agape* transcends all human efforts to love. *Agape* love is a love that gives simply for the joy of giving. It's a love that chooses to sacrifice. It's God's love, first received by you through faith, and then coming out of you to bless another. The truth is that the real level of your maturity can be known by the measure of your love.

So take a moment and allow for some personal reflection. How mature is your love? How much does God's love inform your perspective and influence the way you talk and act? Are you aware of his love throughout the day, coming to you and flowing from you? Is it possible that you've built a good Christian life but may still be a novice in the area of love?

The discipleship model outlined in this book can be understood only in the context of *agape*. Without growth in love, these habits are another list of to-dos. But when they are understood through the lens of *agape*, they lead to profound spiritual growth. Reflect on the seven spiritual habits we have explored:

- Habit 1: Spend the first hour of your morning alone with God.
- Habit 2: Share your faith every week.
- Habit 3: Obey the daily promptings of the Holy Spirit.
- Habit 4: Live within the accountability of biblical sexual boundaries.
- Habit 5: Structure your life around priority, percentage, and progressive giving.
- Habit 6: Practice living by grace through a weekly Sabbath routine.
- Habit 7: Build an intentional circle of discipleship.

Now consider each habit through the lens of growth in love.

Habit 1: Relationship. *Receive* the love of God daily by seeking him in the morning. Remind your soul that the greatest treasure in life is not what God gives, but God himself. Allow your heart to internalize the truth that, in Christ, you are the beloved.

Habit 2: Radiance. Learn to *give* the love you have freely received by stepping out of your comfort zone and sharing Christ with others. Show kindness to the stranger. Take time to listen to those whom God brings across your path. Pray for a heart that loves others, and grow your heart of love by sharing your faith.

Habit 3: Receptivity. *Abide* in love throughout the day, learning to depend on his Spirit for guidance and direction. Don't try to earn the ability to hear the Spirit. Instead, learn to rest in the confidence that God is with you because of grace.

Habit 4: Righteousness. Grow in holiness as you *obey* love, and surrender your natural desires to his design for your sexuality. Experience the greater power of Christ in you to live beyond lust and temptation.

Habit 5: Resources. Grow your *trust* in love by practicing financial generosity. As you give God control of your resources, your confidence in his love for you grows.

Habit 6: Rhythm. *Submit* to love by practicing a weekly Sabbath. Through this habit, learn to freely receive love rather than trying to earn it. Rest in God's satisfaction toward you instead of in your list of personal achievements.

Habit 7: Replication. *Stretch* your love by investing your best in someone else, and experience the joy of seeing that person grow. This will allow you to break the power of selfishness and celebrate the success of another.

The essence of these seven habits is not to make you a really good person. Rather, they are to give you a practical strategy to grow in love. Through these habits you will learn *to receive love, give love, abide in love, obey love, trust in love, submit to love, and stretch love.*

This has been God's strategy for spiritual growth all along. "From him the whole body, joined and held together by every supporting ligament, grows and *builds itself up in love*, as each part does its work" (Ephesians 4:16 NIV).

One last question: What are you waiting for?

Are you waiting for a perfect mentor to model all of this for you? Unfortunately, you may wait the rest of your life. If you feel alone, like no one else around you is taking their spiritual growth this seriously, then God wants to start a spiritual awakening through *you*.

Begin by gathering a few other hungry people and building the flesh-and-blood model together. Don't wait for perfect circumstances. Don't wait for someone else to lead the way. We live in a world where everyone wants change but no one wants to take the first step. You need to take it. Albert Schweitzer said, "The tragedy of life is what dies inside a man while he still lives." Don't let the most important dream in life—getting close to God—die in you. Take action now. Meet with your pastor or church leadership, and begin the journey together. Start taking steps to grow today.

Begin with baby steps. You will never perfectly live these seven habits. No one outside of Jesus ever has. There will always be room for growth because there is always more room for love. But it's time to take out the shovel and bury your ordinary. Bury that old way of unintentional spiritual growth. Once you start, you won't want to go back to the routines of ordinary. You can't meander and wander any longer, hoping to one day reach maturity. For too long we have lived without a real actionable plan for spiritual growth. Now, hopefully, the next step is clear. What will you do?

I'm asking God for a *new ordinary*. And together, who knows what's possible. Maybe you are the one God will use to spark the next great spiritual awakening.

ASSESSMENT TOOL FOR SPIRITUAL GROWTH

This assessment tool gives you a practical way to monitor your growth in each of the seven spiritual habits. Use this tool every three months to reflect on your spiritual growth and isolate areas of focus for the future. On a scale of 1 to 10, with 1 being "never true of me" and 10 being "always true of me," rate where you fall in each area.

Habit 1: Relationship

I devote an hour every morning to seeking God.

1   2   3   4   5   6   7   8   9   10

I practically apply the Bible weekly.

1   2   3   4   5   6   7   8   9   10

I enjoy and look forward to prayer.

1   2   3   4   5   6   7   8   9   10

I sense the love of God toward me throughout my day.

1   2   3   4   5   6   7   8   9   10

I am growing in my knowledge of Scripture.

1   2   3   4   5   6   7   8   9   10

I am growing in my love for God.

1   2   3   4   5   6   7   8   9   10

I approach my time with God each day with a sense of expectation.

1   2   3   4   5   6   7   8   9   10

Habit 2: Radiance

I regularly pray for people who are far from God.

1   2   3   4   5   6   7   8   9   10

I live each day aware of the reality of heaven and hell.

1   2   3   4   5   6   7   8   9   10

I live each week as though I care about the lost.

1   2   3   4   5   6   7   8   9   10

I engage in a spiritual conversation with people far from God every week.

1   2   3   4   5   6   7   8   9   10

I recognize opportunities throughout each week to share Christ.

1   2   3   4   5   6   7   8   9   10

I invite people to church regularly.

1   2   3   4   5   6   7   8   9   10

I am living with a holy sense of urgency.

1   2   3   4   5   6   7   8   9   10

Habit 3: Receptivity

I create space in my heart and life to listen for God's guidance.

1   2   3   4   5   6   7   8   9   10

I live spiritually confident, free from an inner sense of condemnation.

1   2   3   4   5   6   7   8   9   10

I keep track of the impressions God's Spirit has been giving me.

1   2   3   4   5   6   7   8   9   10

I live with a confident sense of God's will for my life.

1   2   3   4   5   6   7   8   9   10

I expect God to speak to me throughout the day.

1   2   3   4   5   6   7   8   9   10

I regularly ask God to speak to me.

1   2   3   4   5   6   7   8   9   10

I live each day available to God.

1   2   3   4   5   6   7   8   9   10

Habit 4: Righteousness

I regularly turn to God as my ultimate source of identity.

1   2   3   4   5   6   7   8   9   10

I have allowed God's view of sexuality to reframe my perspective.

1   2   3   4   5   6   7   8   9   10

I am living habitually free from destructive sexual habits.

1   2   3   4   5   6   7   8   9   10

I take sexual sin as seriously as God takes it.

1   2   3   4   5   6   7   8   9   10

I am living from a posture of dependence, deeply aware of my own brokenness.

1   2   3   4   5   6   7   8   9   10

I am living with honest, transparent accountability in my life.

1   2   3   4   5   6   7   8   9   10

I regularly access and depend on the resurrection power of Christ to say no to lust.

1   2   3   4   5   6   7   8   9   10

Habit 5: Resources

I intentionally forsake wealth as a source of safety, security, and status, because I find these things in Christ.

1   2   3   4   5   6   7   8   9   10

I live as a steward rather than as an owner.

1   2   3   4   5   6   7   8   9   10

I trust God more with my money today than I did a month ago.

1   2   3   4   5   6   7   8   9   10

I see a deep desire in myself to be more generous.

1   2   3   4   5   6   7   8   9   10

I set aside money to give first before spending on anything else.

1   2   3   4   5   6   7   8   9   10

I intentionally give a specific percentage of everything I earn.

1   2   3   4   5   6   7   8   9   10

I have increased my overall giving in the last year.

1   2   3   4   5   6   7   8   9   10

Habit 6: Rhythm

I am living free from the false virtue of ceaseless activity.

1   2   3   4   5   6   7   8   9   10

I find my value in Christ above my performance.

1   2   3   4   5   6   7   8   9   10

I take a twenty-four-hour Sabbath each week.

1   2   3   4   5   6   7   8   9   10

I live confidently aware that God is satisfied with me.
1   2   3   4   5   6   7   8   9   10

I take time to plan my activities before the Sabbath day comes.
1   2   3   4   5   6   7   8   9   10

I intentionally pause, pray, and play during my Sabbath time.
1   2   3   4   5   6   7   8   9   10

I deeply enjoy and look forward to the weekly gift of Sabbath.
1   2   3   4   5   6   7   8   9   10

Habit 7: Replication

I have more mature and less mature people in my life whom I regularly meet with for the purpose of spiritual growth.
1   2   3   4   5   6   7   8   9   10

I have someone in my life whom I am reaching out to and challenging in his or her personal spiritual growth.
1   2   3   4   5   6   7   8   9   10

I regularly initiate spiritually challenging conversations with others.
1   2   3   4   5   6   7   8   9   10

I plan to continue walking closely with a small group of spiritually hungry believers, because I see the value in this.
1   2   3   4   5   6   7   8   9   10

I am experiencing the joy of playing a role in the spiritual growth of another.

1   2   3   4   5   6   7   8   9   10

I can point to a growing number of people whom I am discipling.

1   2   3   4   5   6   7   8   9   10

I am carefully growing as a disciple-maker, taking inventory of my heart and motives.

1   2   3   4   5   6   7   8   9   10

Results: Individually add up your scores from each of the seven sections and divide the total number from each section by seven. You should have seven numbers—one number for each habit. Use the following guide to assess your growth in each habit:

Average score of 1–3: This habit has not taken root in your life. Invite someone who is strong in this area to walk alongside you. Together, create some specific, tangible spiritual goals. Take this assessment again in three months.

Average score of 4–6: This habit is on autopilot. It's time to give it some intentional development. Look for a friend who is also in this range, and challenge each other over the next six weeks. Talk at least weekly about your progress.

Average score of 7–10: This is a real strength in your spiritual life. Ask yourself, "How can I mature in love through this habit? Where do I have action without deep heart affection?" Find someone who is scoring lower in this habit and invest time regularly in helping that person to grow.

NOTES

1. Martin Luther, quoted in Kathleen Burnett, "Twenty Martin Luther Quotes—500 Years Later," Casting My Net, October 16, 2017, www.castingmynet.com/20-martin -luther-quotes-500-years-later/.

2. Derek Walker, ed., *Animated Architecture* (London: Academy Editions, 1982), 10.

3. David Dalton, *James Dean: The Mutant King, a Biography* (Chicago: A Cappella Books, 1974), 342.

4. Dennis Hevesi, "Victor Dorman, 80, Who Altered the Packaging of Cheese, Dies," *New York Times*, March 12, 1995, 47.

5. *The Confessions of St. Augustine: Modern English Version* (Grand Rapids, MI: Baker, 2008), 15–16.

6. Jim Collins, *Good to Great: Why Some Companies Make the Leap and Others Don't* (New York: HarperCollins, 2001), 127.

7. H. Norman Gardiner, introduction to *Selected Sermons of Jonathan Edwards* (New York: Macmillan Company, 1904), x.

8. James Clear, "How Your Habits Shape Your Identity (and Vice Versa)," ch. 3 in *Atomic Habits: Tiny Changes, Remarkable Results* (New York: Avery, 2018), 29–42.

9. Henry Cloud and John Townsend, *How People Grow: What the Bible Reveals about Personal Growth* (Grand Rapids, MI: Zondervan, 2001), 147.

10. Timothy J. Keller, "The Call to Discipleship: Luke 9:20–25, 51–62," C. S. Lewis Institute, from *Knowing and Doing*, winter 2011, accessed July 21, 2020, www.cslewisinstitute.org/The_Call_To_Discipleship_SinglePage.

11. Thomas Chalmers, "The Expulsive Power of a New Affection," sermon, quoted in Keller, "Call to Discipleship," 5.

12. John McLean, "The Printing Revolution, Western Civilization," Lumen Learning, accessed January 21, 2020, https://courses.lumenlearning.com/suny-hccc-worldhistory /chapter/the-printing-revolution/.

13. Albert Bandura, *Social Learning Theory* (New York: General Learning Press, 1977), 22.

14. D. L. Moody, *The Overcoming Life and Other Sermons* (Chicago: Bible Institute Colportage, Revell, 1896), 17.

15. Brennan Manning, *Abba's Child: The Cry of the Heart for Intimate Belonging* (Colorado Springs: NavPress, 2015), 34.

16. Alicia Britt Chole, *Anonymous: Jesus' Hidden Years … and Yours* (Nashville, TN: Thomas Nelson, 2006), 32.

17. Jacopo Prisco, "Illusion of Control: Why the World Is Full of Buttons That Don't Work," CNN, September 3, 2018, www.cnn.com/style/article/placebo-buttons-design /index.html.

18. A. W. Tozer, *The Knowledge of the Holy: The Attributes of God, Their Meaning in the Christian Life* (New York: HarperCollins, 1961), 1.

19. C. Austin Miles, "In the Garden," hymn, 1912, Hymnary.org, accessed January 21, 2020, https://hymnary.org/text/i_come_to_the_garden_alone.

20. Malcolm Gladwell, *Outliers: The Story of Success* (New York: Little, Brown and Company, 2008), 40.

21. Tony Reinke, "The New Tolerance Must Crumble, Says Don Carson," Desiring God, January 28, 2016, www.desiringgod.org/articles/the-new-tolerance-must-crumble -says-don-carson.

22. Timothy Keller, "Reading 7—Witness," sermon, in *A Vision for a Gospel-Centered Life*, Monergism, accessed July 21, 2020, www.monergism.com/sites/default/files /manual/ebooks/vision-gospel.pdf.

23. C. S. Lewis, *The Four Loves* (New York: HarperCollins, 1960), 155.

24. Louis Menand, "When Martin Luther King, Jr., Became a Leader," *New Yorker*, April 4, 2018, www.newyorker.com/news/daily-comment/when-martin-luther-king-jr -became-a-leader.

25. Peter F. Gunther, comp., *Sermon Classics by Great Preachers* (Chicago: Moody, 1982), 7–10.

26. Dallas Willard, *Hearing God: Developing a Conversational Relationship with God* (Downers Grove, IL: InterVarsity, 2012), 137.

27. Brother Lawrence, *The Practice of the Presence of God: The Best Rule of Holy Life* (Peabody, MA: Hendrickson, 2004), 42.

28. A. T. Pierson, *George Müller of Bristol and His Witness to a Prayer-Hearing God* (New York: Baker and Taylor, 1899), 185–86.

29. *The Way In Is the Way On: John Wimber's Teachings and Writings on Christ* (Boise, ID: Ampelon, 2006), 217.

30. Henry Cloud and John Townsend, *Boundaries: When to Say Yes, How to Say No to Take Control of Your Life* (Grand Rapids, MI: Zondervan, 1992), 45.

31. "Ted Haggard's Statement to New Life Church," The Alliance, November 6, 2006, www.cmalliance.org/news/2006/11/06/ted-haggards-statement-to-new-life-church/.

32. John Eldredge, *Wild at Heart: Discovering the Secret of a Man's Soul* (Nashville, TN: Thomas Nelson, 2001), 115.

33. "Porn Profits: Corporate America's Secret," ABC News, January 6, 2006, https://abcnews.go.com/Primetime/story?id=132001&page=1; Joe Pinsker, "The Hidden Economics of Porn," *Atlantic*, April 4, 2016, www.theatlantic.com/business /archive/2016/04/pornography-industry-economics-tarrant/476580/; and "Porn Industry Archives," Enough Is Enough, accessed October 8, 2020, https://enough.org /stats_porn_industry_archives.

34. Grant Hilary Brenner, "When Is Porn Use a Problem?," *Psychology Today*, February 19, 2018, www.psychologytoday.com/us/blog/experimentations/201802/when-is-porn -use-problem#:~:text=In%20terms%20of%20basic%20results,and%2026%20percent %20of%20women.

35. Manning, *Abba's Child*, 5.

36. "Water, Sanitation, and Hygiene," UNICEF, accessed July 22, 2020, www.unicef .org/wash/.

37. "Global Wealth Report 2019," Credit Suisse Research Institute, www.credit-suisse .com/about-us/en/reports-research/global-wealth-report.html, 10.

38. Daniel Kurt, "Are You in the Top 1 Percent of the World?," Investopedia, November 18, 2019, www.investopedia.com/articles/personal-finance/050615/are-you -top-one-percent-world.asp.

39. John Eldredge, interview by Dick Staub, "John Eldredge Is Wild at Heart," *Christianity Today*, November 1, 2003, www.christianitytoday.com/ct/2003 /novemberweb-only/11-10-21.0.html?share=.

40. C. S. Lewis, *The Chronicles of Narnia Volume III: The Voyage of the Dawn Treader* (Hong Kong: Enrich Spot, 2016), 77–78.

41. Augustine, *On Christian Teaching*, trans. R. P. H. Green (Oxford: Oxford University Press, 1997), 21.

42. Lance Witt, *Replenish: Leading from a Healthy Soul* (Grand Rapids, MI: Baker Books, 2011), 74–75.

43. Henri J. M. Nouwen, *In the Name of Jesus: Reflections on Christian Leadership* (Chestnut Ridge, NY: Crossroad, 2002), 20.

44. Peter Scazzero, *The Emotionally Healthy Leader: How Transforming Your Inner Life Will Deeply Transform Your Church, Team, and the World* (Grand Rapids, MI: Zondervan, 2015), 25.

45. "Stress Research," American Institute of Stress, accessed July 22, 2020, www.stress .org/stress-research.

46. Scazzero, *Emotionally Healthy Leader*, 55.

47. Manning, *Abba's Child*, 34.

48. Henri J. M. Nouwen, *You Are the Beloved: Daily Meditations for Spiritual Living* (New York: Convergent Books, 2017), 12.

49. Wayne Muller, *Sabbath: Finding Rest, Renewal, and Delight in Our Busy Lives* (New York: Bantam Books, 1999), 82.

50. Dallas Willard, *The Great Omission: Reclaiming Jesus's Essential Teachings on Discipleship* (New York: HarperCollins, 2006), 36.

51. Dietrich Bonhoeffer, *The Cost of Discipleship* (New York: Touchstone, 1995), 89.

52. "Flesh and Blood" by Johnny Cash, track 1 on *I Walk the Line* (soundtrack), Columbia Records, 1970.

53. Epictetus, *Discourses and Selected Writings*, trans. Robert Dobbin (London: Penguin Books, 2008), n.p.

54. Stephen E. Ambrose, *Citizen Soldiers: The US Army from the Normandy Beaches to the Bulge to the Surrender of Germany* (New York: Touchstone, 1997), 73.

55. Robert E. Coleman, *The Master Plan of Evangelism* (Grand Rapids, MI: Revell, 1993), 109.

56. Coleman, *Master Plan of Evangelism*, 32.

57. Wayne Cordeiro, *Sifted: Pursuing Growth through Trials, Challenges, and Disappointments* (Grand Rapids, MI: Zondervan, 2012), 74.

58. "The Resolutions of Jonathan Edwards," Desiring God, December 30, 2006, www.desiringgod.org/articles/the-resolutions-of-jonathan-edwards.

59. "Love More Excellent Than the Extraordinary Gifts of the Spirit by Jonathan Edwards (1703–1758)," Bible Bulletin Board, accessed January 22, 2020, www.biblebb.com/files/edwards/charity2.htm.